EDITOR: MARTIN

ELITE S

AFRIKAKOR

CW00918345

Text by
GORDON WILLIAMSON
Colour plates by
RON VOLSTAD

Published in 1991 by
Osprey Publishing Ltd
59 Grosvenor Street, London, W1X 9DA
© Copyright 1991 Osprey Publishing Ltd

British Library Cataloguing in Publication Data

Williamson, Gordon
  Afrikakorps 1941–43. – (Elite, 34).
  1. Africa. Armies, history
  I. Title   II. Volstad, Ron   III. Series
  356.0961

  ISBN 1-85532-130-0

Filmset in Great Britain by Keyspools Ltd, Golborne,
Lancs
Printed through Bookbuilders Ltd, Hong Kong

Author's Note
The term 'Afrikakorps' strictly speaking refers to only
a small element of the entire German forces in North
Africa. However, the term is now popularly used to
refer to all of Rommel's German forces.

Acknowledgements
I would like to express my sincere thanks to the
following for their assistance in the preparation of this
work: Josef Charita, Malcolm Bowers, Daniel Rose,
Arthur Charlton, Paul Anderson, Ewan Lindsay,
Derek Crawford.

INTRODUCTION

So many battles of the Second World War were fought with such ferocity and disregard for basic humanity that many survivors of that time have only the most bitter memories of their wartime experiences. The campaign in North Africa between September 1940 and May 1943 holds not only an enduring fascination for postwar generations; but also a perhaps unique degree of nostalgia for some surviving participants. The campaign was no less costly in terms of human lives and material than many others; but regret at the cost is accompanied by positive memories in the minds of many veterans. This is not to suggest that the dead have been forgotten; but an almost mystical bond nevertheless exists, even between former enemies, amongst veterans of the desert campaign. Their memories seem to have a special quality not found among men who fought on other fronts, and enduring hatred is very rarely voiced.

This can in some ways be explained by a number of contributory factors. Firstly there is the mystique of the desert itself. This was a vividly inhospitable battlefield, where the scorching, arid terrain by day became an equally unwelcoming, freezing world at night; where raging sandstorms could completely alter a landscape within just a few hours; and where countless flies, scorpions and sand vipers, to say nothing of open sores, jaundice and dysentery, could make life a complete misery. Soldiers of both sides suffered equally in this merciless environment, a factor which would certainly engender a common bond.

Secondly, by virtue of the inhospitable terrain, the population of this part of the world is sparse; civilian casualties were light, and the combatants were usually spared the moral dilemmas inseparable from the conduct of war in densely inhabited regions.

The men of both Rommel's Afrikakorps and the British 8th Army came to feel part of an élite, and

'The Desert Fox': Generalfeldmarschall Erwin Rommel, 1942. He wears the field grey and dark green Schirmmütze, with gold general officer's distinctions, from the continental uniform (a phrase used throughout this book to identify the regulation European clothing of the German forces). The tunic is that of a fine-quality lightweight tobacco brown wool tropical uniform, as privately acquired by senior officers and instantly recognisable by its open collar. At the throat Rommel wears his Knight's Cross with Swords and Oakleaves, and the Pour le Mérite awarded for gallantry in Italy in the Great War. Photos show that as a rule Rommel wore only these orders, his tunic being devoid of decorations.

both sides developed a sense of esprit de corps second to none, born partly of their long experience of mastering an isolated environment which demanded total self-reliance from European armies.

Last but not least was the fact that almost without exception, the war in the desert was fought 'cleanly', and there are countless tales of humanitarian acts on both sides. The desert campaign was almost unique in this relative freedom from atrocity. Both sides were commanded by officers of the highest calibre, men who had the greatest respect for their opponent's capabilities—as indeed did the individual soldiers of each army.

Countless books have appeared on the subject of the campaign in North Africa from both sides. To cover all aspects of the battles, the commanders, the equipment, uniforms and insignia would require a massive work of many volumes. This small book will restrict itself to providing the reader with a basic background knowledge of the Afrikakorps, its organisation, uniforms and insignia. For those who wish to study the subject in greater depth there are numerous specialist works available; amongst the best are: *Uniforms, Organisation & History of the Afrikakorps* by R. J. Bender and R. D. Law (Bender Publishing); *Rommel* by R. D. Law and C. W. H. Luther (Bender Publishing); and *Rommel's Army in Africa* by Dal McGuirk (Century Hutchison Ltd).

THE CAMPAIGN

German military involvement in North Africa was brought about as a gesture of support by Hitler for his incompetent ally Mussolini. The Italians, eager to share in Hitler's continuing military success, had invaded Egypt from their colony of Libya in September 1940, outnumbering the meagre British forces by some five to one. During the first major engagements, which began when the British Commander, Middle East Forces, Gen. Wavell, launched his originally limited 'Compass' offensive on 9 December, the Italians were dealt a severe blow to their strength and morale, losing vast numbers of prisoners. After the battle of Sidi Barrani, when the retreating Italian forces were cut off at Buq Buq, their losses stood at 38,000 compared with 624 among the British Commonwealth troops.

German reconnaissance troops parade in Tripoli, February 1941; these motorcycle crews are probably from the recce battalion of 5th Light Division, Aufkl.-Abt.(mot) 3. They wear full regulation tropical dress including the unpopular pith helmet.

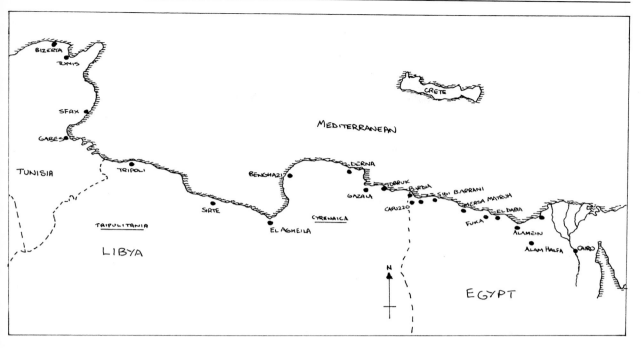

The Italians were pursued into Libya where a major force of some 45,000 was besieged at the fortresss of Bardia by the Australians, surrendering on 5 January 1941 after their commander, Gen. Berganzoli, had left his men to their fate. The Italian commander fled to Tobruk where defences were hurriedly strengthened. On 21 January the allies attacked with scant but effective armoured support; and after a short but bitterly fought battle Berganzoli once again fled, leaving over 27,000 men of his garrison to surrender. Although near to exhaustion, the smaller Commonwealth force pursued the Italians relentlessly until, on 7 February, the enemy surrendered at Beda Fomm. Mussolini had lost a total of over 130,000 men and 380 tanks in just two months.

Hitler had offered Mussolini his assistance in the form of a German Panzer Division prior to the Italian invasion of Egypt, but the overconfident Italian dictator had declined. Now it seemed that without immediate German support the Italians would soon be driven out of North Africa altogether. The die was now cast and German involvement in the desert war was inevitable. Gen. O'Connor's Western Desert Force (from 1 January 1941, XIII Corps) of some 31,000 British and Commonwealth troops of 7th Armoured Division and 4th Indian Division, rein-forced by 6th Australian Division and New Zealand troops, had decisively defeated the Italian 5th and 10th Armies, comprising some 236,000 men. Now, however, they would face an entirely different calibre of troops and commanders.

Rommel's first campaign, February 1941

The first German units arrived in Tripolis on 14 February 1941; they comprised advance echelon troops of 5 leichte Division and 3 Panzer Regiment as well as support units such as pioneers and reconnaissance troops. Fully motorised and with good quality armour, the German force was small but powerful. It was commanded by Generalleutnant Erwin Rommel, a respected and able soldier who had gained a high reputation during the campaign in France, where he commanded 7 Panzer Division.

Due to the perilous situation in Libya the German force was committed to the front immediately, and anti-tank defences were constructed. Ger-

DAK Panzer III tanks parade through an Italian colonial town. The arrival of modern armour, led by an energetic commander, transformed the desert war, which in winter 1940 had been an unbroken succession of British victories.

man reconnaissance troops soon established contact with the enemy, and before long Rommel became aware of the extent to which British forces had been overstretched and weakened by the exhausting if victorious campaign against the Italians. In addition, Wavell had lost some of his British armour and Australian and New Zealand troops to the campaign in Greece, and 4th Indian Division to Ethiopia.

Rommel, living up to his reputation of missing no opportunity to strike at the enemy when the situation favoured him, struck towards the strategic supply port of Tobruk, attacking the British forces at El Agheila. The tide turned against the British as the fresh troops of Rommel's Afrikakorps pushed them back toward Mersa Brega. Despite orders not to undertake any ambitious major operations at this stage, Rommel decided to press home his advantage; part of 5 leichte Division was despatched up the coast towards Benghazi while his Panzers, and the remainder of 5 leichte, pushed on across the desert to El Mechili.

On 4 April 1941 Benghazi fell, followed three days later by El Mechili; and one of Rommel's patrol units capturing Lt. Gen. Richard O'Connor and Gen. Neame. O'Connor was one of the best British field commanders at this stage in the war and his loss was a severe blow to the exhausted British forces. The bulk of 2nd Armoured Division were captured as Rommel relentlessly pursued his retreating enemy back towards Tobruk.

Tobruk itself was to be a different matter, however. With a strong garrison force of some 35,000 men including Australian troops of the inexperienced but determined 9th Division, Wavell was under orders to hold Tobruk at all costs. Even if cut off he could be resupplied by sea, as the Royal Navy still had control of the Mediterranean. Rommel's attack on this powerful garrison had little effect, particularly as he had divided his forces, sending some units on ahead to secure Fort Capuzzo, Halfaya Pass and Sollum. His first attack on Tobruk was made by Pioniere, a Maschinen-Gewehre Bataillon and some elements of 5 Panzer Regiment. Despite the failure of the attack on Tobruk, however, Rommel had succeeded in driving the British out of Cyrenaica in just 12 days.

'Brevity' and 'Battleaxe', May–June 1941

In mid-May Wavell launched Operation 'Brevity' in an attempt to recapture the frontier positions at Halfaya, Sollum and Capuzzo. These were taken, but the British were thrown out again just ten days later. In mid-June Wavell was persuaded by Churchill to launch another attack to relieve the Tobruk garrison and, reinforced by a large shipment of tanks and fighter aircraft, he launched Operation 'Battleaxe' on 15 June. Wavell's forces attempted to encircle the German positions at Halfaya and attack from the rear. This offensive lasted only three days. The British were shocked at the strong defence offered by the Axis forces at Halfaya, where the deadly 88 mm Flak guns were used in their equally effective anti-tank rôle. By 16 June Rommel's counter-attack had halted the British and began to roll them back. By 17 June the British had been pushed back into Egypt

and the encircled Halfaya garrison relieved. British losses were heavy, with 91 tanks destroyed for the loss of only 12 Panzers. On 21 June Wavell was relieved, and passed his command to Gen. Auchinleck.

Following this ill-fated British offensive there was a period of several months of relative inactivity while both sides rebuilt their battered forces, Auchinleck preparing for yet another offensive to relieve Tobruk and Rommel establishing formidable defensive positions. The garrison at Tobruk continued to be supplied by sea. While the Axis were stronger in air power, the British still enjoyed naval superiority; at one stage as much as 62% of the Axis supply convoys were being lost to Allied attacks.

'Crusader', November 1941

Rommel determined to launch yet another attack on Tobruk on 20 November. The Allies, however, were aware of Rommel's plans, principally through the 'Ultra' interception of coded radio traffic, and had precise details of Axis strength and positions. Auchinleck launched his own offensive, Operation 'Crusader', two days before Rommel's own planned attack on Tobruk, catching the Axis forces unawares. The British planned a sweep up through the desert in the area between the Egyptian frontier and Tobruk cutting off the Axis positions at Halfaya and Bardia and providing a launch point for the relief of Tobruk. British reinforcements had been arriving at a regular

A medal award ceremony in the field. The troops wear the peaked field cap apart from the two honour guards, wearing steel helmets. All ranks seem to wear the high lace-up tropical boot. (Josef Charita)

Panzer III tank crew in tropical shirts and shorts, two of them still wearing the black Feldmütze of continental uniform, the others peaked tropical field caps. At left note high laced boots; also a captured South African pith helmet, badged with German insignia.

rate until, now, on the eve of the offensive, Auchinleck could field 736 tanks to Rommel's 240 Panzers; Rommel also had some 150 Italian tanks but these were generally of such dubious quality that they could hardly be held to be a significant factor.

Operation 'Crusader' began on 18 November 1941 when the newly redesignated 8th Army, commanded by Lt. Gen. Cunningham and comprising XIII and XXX Corps, poured over the border. Opposing them were the Italian Ariete and Trieste Divisions in the Italian XX Mobile Corps and the German Panzergruppe Afrika, comprising the Deutsches Afrikakorps and the Italian XXI Corps. The Afrikakorps itself included the Italian Savona Division as well as 15 and 21 Panzer Divisions and 90 leichte Afrika Division.

The troops on Cunningham's right flank made good progress, with XIII Corps (the New Zealand and 4th Indian Divisions and 1st Army Tank Brigade) hooking around Sidi Omar towards Bardia. On the desert flank, however, XXX Corps (7th Armoured and 1st South African Divs., 4th Armoured and 22nd Guards Bdes.) failed to draw the Panzers into battle and became vulnerably dispersed. At Bir el Gubi 7th Armoured lost some 50 tanks to the stout defenders from Ariete Division. Cunningham's left flank forces eventually took Sidi Rezegh, only to be pushed back again by a massive

Axis counter-attack when Rommel's Panzer Divisions smashed into the British XXX Corps from two directions. The British lost over 200 tanks.

The 'Crusader' battles see-sawed back and forth in three weeks of furious combat, with many targets being captured and lost several times. Just as the tide seemed to turn against the British, Rommel led a major part of his force racing towards the Egyptian frontier, hoping to cut off the British and attack from the rear. Whilst Rommel, with some 100 Panzers, rampaged around the British rear, isolated from the main battle and unable to draw the enemy into battle, the British grimly fought on. By drawing off such a large part of his mobile forces Rommel had surrendered control of large areas he had fought hard to win. By the time he realised that his 'Dash to the Wire' had failed and returned to his headquarters, the battle was once again beginning to turn against him. The Tobruk garrison had started to strike out eastwards, and on 26 November, New Zealand troops from XIII Corps met up with the Tobruk veterans at El Duda. Although the battle produced no outright winner, British losses (18,000 casualties and 287 tanks, against Axis losses of 30,000 and over 300) could easily be made up, while German resupply was becoming more problematic by the day and would continue to do so as long as the Royal Navy controlled the Mediterranean. On 6 December, therefore, Rommel broke off the action and pulled his forces back from Cyrenaica to the Tripolitanian border, eventually forming a new front line back at El Agheila at the beginning of January 1942.

All was not lost, however. Japan had entered the war, and the sudden need for both manpower and materiel in the Far East robbed Auchinleck of much-needed supplies and reinforcement. Additionally, winter conditions on the Russian Front had curtailed the bulk of the Luftwaffe's combat flying, allowing the temporary transfer of considerable air strength for the North African front.

January–June 1942: Rommel rebounds

By mid-January 1942 Rommel was sufficiently re-supplied to plan a new offensive before the now over-extended British could catch their breath. On 21 January Italian forces drove hard to Benghazi, whilst the Germans pushed the British back 'across the bulge' to Mechili and thence on to a line south from Gazala. At this point both sides dug in, Rommel being disinclined to stretch his supply lines any further at this stage.

Once again a quiet few months ensued while both sides built up their strength. Rommel was the first to reach preparedness, though the build-up of British forces at Gazala forced him into action earlier than he would have wished. He intended to move on Tobruk, while the Italians took the entrenched position at Bir Hacheim to the south-west, at the desert tip of the allied line.

On 27/28 May 1942, Rommel's Panzers hooked round the left of the British lines and swept north-east to join battle with the 8th Army, slowly gaining the upper hand in fierce combat. To the south, however, the Free French forces holding Bir Hacheim rebuffed all Italian attempts to capture the fortress. Rommels' supplies ran low, and a combin-

Rommel himself rarely wore shorts; this photo was taken in August 1942 near El Alamein.

Oberstleutnant Crasemann discusses a situation map with Rommel, June 1942. Even senior ranks often wore the casual and comfortable shirtsleeve-and-shorts uniform; note socks rolled over ankle boots. (Josef Charita)

A smiling Luftwaffe mechanic, wearing the blue-grey Fliegermütze from the continental uniform, sits on the cowling of a Junkers Ju87B Stuka. Note the neatly painted Luftwaffe variation of the DAK's palm-and-swastika insignia. (Josef Charita)

garrison area and the remainder withdrawing south towards the frontier with Egypt. After only a few days' respite Rommel's men were thrown into the battle for Tobruk. The Germans were well acquainted with Tobruk's defences and attacked on 20 June from the south-east before the defenders could adequately prepare. On 21 June the garrison, mainly 2nd South African Division, surrendered, thus providing Rommel with a windfall of captured supplies. The British were shocked and demoralised by this unexpected reverse.

A delighted Hitler promoted Rommel to Generalfeldmarschall, the youngest in the German Army. Despite his original intent to halt at Tobruk until the British garrison at Malta was subdued, removing the danger of attacks on his supply convoys, Rommel successfully pressed Hitler for permission to pursue the retreating British into Egypt, and German troops crossed the frontier on 23 June.

Auchinleck moved his reserves into position at Mersah Matruh to block the pursuing Germans. The British could field around 20,000 men, far more than Rommel's mobile spearhead of 21 Panzer and 90 leichte Divisions; despite this, poor command of the British troops and atrocious confusion and lack of communications allowed the Germans to encircle the Mersah Matruh positions. Not realising the weak state of Rommel's forces, the New Zealand Division broke out of Mersah Matruh and retreated eastwards. Nothing now stood between Rommel and Alexandria but for the untested defensive position along a line south from El Alamein. This was, however, an excellent natural defensive position. With the sea to the north and the impassable Quattara Depression to the south, only a narrow strip of land remained to be defended.

On 30 June 1942 German mechanised units hit the first line of defensive minefields. This was to be the start of four months of intensive fighting. Within a few days of the first contact Rommel realised his troops were too exhausted to continue and pulled his forces back to rest and regroup. Italian forces coming up to the line took over the forward positions. The British had no intention of allowing Rommel this respite, however, and throughout July mounted numerous attacks on the German positions. By the end of that month little advantage had been gained by either side and both were exhausted.

ation of minefields and RAF strafing attacks reduced German mobility to a dangerous degree. Both sides were almost exhausted. Had the British been aware of Rommel's precarious position and made an all-out effort at this point, they might have succeeded in destroying the German force. As it was, Rommel despatched 90 leichte Division south, and with the Italian 'Ariete' Division and Luftwaffe support eventually forced the French to abandon Bir Hacheim on 11 June, thus securing his supply routes.

Now the stalemate was over and by mid-June Rommel could concentrate his forces for the attack on Tobruk. As the British withdrew in some disarray with part of 8th Army moving into the Tobruk

September–November 1942: Alam Halfa and Alamein

Rommel, gambling on the arrival of an expected supply convoy, determined on a further attempt to break through the British positions. An attack was launched on 30 August in which Rommel intended to punch through the southern end of the British line and swing up behind their positions. This plan was known to Auchinleck's newly appointed successor as C-in-C Middle East, Gen. Alexander, thanks to 'Ultra' intercepts. The new commander of 8th Army, Gen. Bernard Montgomery, laid a trap for his adversary. Powerful artillery and dug-in tank forces waited along the Alam Halfa ridge; and when the attacking Germans began to run into the well-prepared British minefields and were forced further south nearer the ridge, the trap was sprung. Battered by artillery and tank fire and by attacking RAF fighter-bombers the Germans suffered heavy losses. Rommel, by now suffering from ill-health, faltered and withdrew his forces, still with their morale high and somewhat surprised by their commander's decision. Rommel left for Germany on sick leave on 23 September, leaving orders that while he was gone widespread defensive minefields be constructed, covered by the superb 88 mm Flak guns. Montgomery resisted political pressure to attack at once, while building up his strength with reinforcements and supplies.

On 23 October, while Rommel was still in Germany, Montgomery launched his anticipated offensive with a ferocious barrage along the entire front line. As the 8th Army advanced into the well-prepared German northern defences progress was slow but determined. When Rommel returned on 25 October he found his men to be in good spirits and holding the line. Knowing Rommel's lack of fuel and weakness in reserves, Montgomery determined to draw him into a battle of attrition and wear his forces down by sheer weight of numbers. After five days of combat the British had still not broken through the German lines and had lost over 10,000 casualties; Montgomery knew, however, that Rommel's strength was now desperately low. On 1 November Montgomery suddenly shifted his attack to the southern sector; and on 4 November Rommel's forces finally accepted the inevitable and began to withdraw.

Late June 1942, near Tobruk: Rommel in his favourite SdKfz 250/3 command halftrack 'Greif'. The grenadier at right has a crude helmet cover made from sandbag hessian; the others have helmets painted sand-colour with a matt finish. (Josef Charita)

Tunisia

Only three days later British and American forces landed in Morocco and Algeria in Operation 'Torch'. Rommel's forces were now trapped between two fronts. Only one solution remained for Rommel: to withdraw into Tunisia and attempt a withdrawal to Sicily. Montgomery was reluctant to engage in any risky pincer movements to cut off the retreating Germans, who, though battered, still had considerable fight left in them. Rommel kept out of reach of the pursuit during a skilful withdrawal, reaching the Mareth Line fortifications in February 1943. Meanwhile, on the western Tunisian front, Gens. Nehring and Von Arnim conducted a skilful and aggressive defence in mountainous terrain against the US-British armies advancing from Algeria.

Although Rommel had by now given up any hope of victory in North Africa, circumstances had now in fact begun to favour the Germans. Now it was Montgomery whose supply lines were dangerously stretched. The Germans had now re-established, if only temporarily, air superiority over the Tunisian bridgehead, and reinforcements were being landed. By the end of December 1942 Axis forces in Tunisia had reached a total of some 100,000 men, and reinforcements had included a heavy tank battalion equipped with the formidable new Tiger.

On 14 February Rommel launched an attack to the west on advancing American units. Both 10 and 21 Panzer Divisions smashed into the Americans at Sidi bou Zid, inflicting grievous losses. A counter-attack on the following day was quickly rebuffed. On 20 November Rommel, with 10 and 15 Panzer Divisions, captured the Kasserine Pass, easily rout-

ing the inexperienced US troops opposing him. Within a couple of days, however, Rommel's advance had stalled through lack of resources and continued stiffening of the Allied defence.

Rommel now turned his attention to the British; a plan was drawn up for an attack at Medenine on the Mareth Line. Unfortunately for Rommel, enemy intelligence had once again given them the exact time and place of the German attack. Well-sited British anti-tank guns took a dreadful toll of the Panzers and infantry losses were equally heavy. On 9 March 1943 Rommel was recalled to Germany and was never to return to Africa. His replacement as C-in-C Panzer-armee Afrika was Gen. von Arnim.

All that was now left to him was to fight a delaying action to hold off the inevitable surrender as long as possible. On 12 March 1943 Von Arnim finally capitulated; the desert war was at an end, and 240,000 Axis troops marched into captivity—but also into history. Few defeated forces have gained such un-grudging respect from their enemies as did the men of Rommel's desert army.

MG 34 gunner on watch in a defensive position; his helmet is effectively camouflaged with thick daubs of dried mud. (Josef Charita)

DAK ORGANISATION

Initially known as 'Aufklärungsstab Rommel' when Rommel was informed of his new position on 6 February 1941, the German army in North Africa was renamed 'Deutsches Afrikakorps' when Hitler announced its official formation on 19 February, the original Aufklärungsstab being absorbed into the new command. At this initial stage the Afrikakorps consisted of the following elements:

Generalkommando (the staff element)

5 leichte Division
15 Panzer Division

Support units:

Korpskartenstelle (m) 576 (Corps Map Unit)

Oasen-Bataillon zbV 300 (Specialist Water Unit)

Panzerjäger Abteilung (m) 605 (Anti-Tank Detachment)

I Batterie/Flak Regiment (m) 18

I Batterie/Flak Regiment (m) 33

Flak-Abteilung (m) 606

Nachrichten-Abteilung (m) 475 (Signals Detachment)

Nachschub-Bataillon (m) 572 (Supplies Battalion)

Wasserversorgungs-Bataillon (m) 580 (Water Provisions Units)

Aufklärungs-Kompanie (m) 580 (Recce Company)

Feldersatz-Bataillon 598 (Field Replacement Unit)

Feldersatz-Bataillon 599

Command group in the most typical clothing for senior officers during 1942: peaked field cap, tropical tunic with shirt and tie, tropical breeches and high laced boots. Rommel greets the Italian Gen. Navarini, XXI Corps; immediately right of him are Gens. Gause and Nehring. (Josef Charita)

Use of the field grey continental Schirmmütze in the desert was far from unknown. This is Oberleutnant Dr. Heinz Lotze, who would survive to win the Knight's Cross as a Hauptmann commanding 1 Kompanie,

Panzer-Regt. Kahle on 8 May 1945. He has added the hand-embroidered silver breast eagle from continental uniform to his tropical blouse, but retains the 'all ranks' tropical collar patches.

Bäckerei-Kompanie (m) 554 (Bakery Company)

Korps-Verpflegungslager (m) (Corps Supply Dump)

Feldgendarmerie-Trupp (m) 498 (Military Police)

Feldpostamt (m) (Field Post Office)

Within six months of its formation the Afrikakorps was raised to the status of a Panzergruppe. As well as the original components, the new Panzergruppe Afrika included 90 leichte Division, and had six Italian divisions placed under its command: the 'Ariete', 'Trieste', 'Pavia', 'Bologna', 'Brescia' and 'Sovana' Divisions.

At the end of January 1942 the Panzergruppe was

renamed Panzerarmee Afrika; and in February 1943, two years after its formation, was retitled 1. italienische Armee by an obviously political decision.

In August 1942, at its high point of success, the Axis army in North Africa consisted of the following elements:

Armeeoberkommando
Deutsches Afrikakorps—
   15 Panzer Division
   21 Panzer Division (formerly 5 leichte Div.)
90 leichte Division
164 Infanterie Division
Fallschirmjäger Brigade Ramcke
Italian X Corps—
   Inf. Div. 'Brescia'
   Inf. Div. 'Pavia'
Italian XX Corps—
   Armd. Div. 'Ariete'
   Armd. Div. 'Littorio'
   Motorised Div. 'Trieste'
   Parachute Div. 'Folgore'
Italian XXI Korps—
   Inf. Div. 'Trento'
   Inf. Div. 'Bologna'

Support & subsidiary units:
Brigade Stab zbV (m) 15
Kampfstaffel (m)
Armee-Kartenstelle (m) 575
Stab Kommandeur der Luftwaffe in Libien
Sonderverband (m) 288
Aufklärungs Stab 2 (Heer)
Panzerjäger Abteilung (m) 605
Panzerjäger Abteilung (m) 606
Artillerie Oberkommando 104
Artillerie-Vermessungs-Trupp (m) 721–730
   (Artillery-Survey)
Beobachtungs-Abteilung (m) 11 (Observer Unit)
Flak Abteilung der Luftwaffe (m) 606
Flak Abteilung der Luftwaffe (m) 612
Flak Abteilung der Luftwaffe (m) 617
Flak Abteilung der Luftwaffe (m) 135
Heeres Bau Dienst (m) 73 (Army Construction Unit)
Bau Bataillon 85
1/Landesschützen-Bataillon 278
Nachrichten-Regiment (m) 10
Kurierstaffel
V Heeres-Funkstelle (Army Radio Post)

VI Heeres-Funkstelle
XIII Heeres-Funkstelle
Tripolis Heeres-Funkstelle
Funk-Trupp zbV Afrika
Nachrichten-Zug 937
Nachschub-Regiment 585
Stab Nachschub-Bataillon (m) 619
Entlade-Stab zbV (m) 681 (Bomb Disposal)
Stab-Nachschub-Bataillon zbV (m) 792
Stab-Nachschub-Bataillon zbV (m) 798
Nachschub-Bataillon (m) 148, 149, 529, 532, 533, 902 & 909
Kraftfahrzeuginstandsetzungs-Abteilung (m) 548 (vehicle maintenance)
Munitionsverwaltungs-Zug (m) 542–547
Betriebssftoffverwaltungs-Zug (m) 12
Heeres-Betriebsstoffverwaltungs-Zug (m) 5
Betriebsstoffverwaltungs-Zug (m) 979–981
Geräte-Verwaltungsdienst (m)
Heeres-Kraftfahr Park (m) 560 & 566
Feldzeugdienst-Zug (m) 1–3 (Field Quartermaster)
1/Bäckerie-Kompanie (m) 554
Schlächterei-Kompanie (m) 445 (Butchery Company)
Verpflegungsamt (m) 317 (Provisions Office)
Verpflegungsamt (m) 445

Verpflegungsamt (m) Afrika
2. Sanitäts Kompanie (m) 592 (Medical Company)
1. Krankentransport-Kompanie (m) 705 (Ambulance Company)
Tripolis Kriegslazarett (m) (Military Hospital)
5/Kriegslazarett (m) 542
Kreigslazarett (m) 667
Leichtkrankenkriegslazarett (m) (Hospital for lightly wounded)
Sanitätspark (m) 531
Geheime-Feldpolizei (m) (Secret Field Police)
Haupt-Streifendeinst (Main Patrol Service)
Feldgendarmerie-Trupp (m)
Wach-Bataillon Afrika (Guard Battalion)
Ortskommandantur Misurata (Local Command)
Ortskommandantur Barce
Ortskommandantur Tripolis
Ortskommandantur Benghazi
Ortskommandantur Derna
Tripolis-Lager Kommandeur

Italian M13/40 tanks of X Tank Bn. near Mechili, March 1942. Throughout his campaigns Rommel was forced to rely on the Italian Army for much of his armour; even at El Alamein 259 of his available total of 497 were out-of-date Italian types, easy prey for enemy weapons.

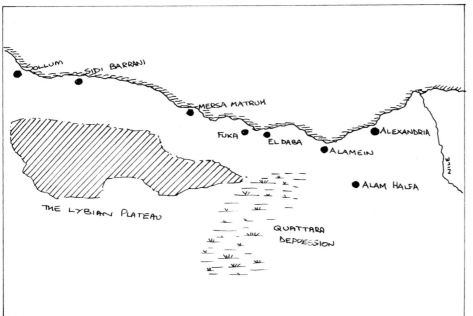

The furthest extent of Rommel's advance eastwards, halted at the line constructed by Auchinleck and Montgomery south from El Alamein. Denied room to manoeuvre by the Quattara Depression, and means to do so by his long and vulnerable supply lines across the Mediterranean, his forces were relentlessly pounded into withdrawal in October–November 1942. Even so, the DAK conducted a masterly retreat up the coastal corridor, and avoided further destruction.

Kriegsgefangenen-Durchgangslager 782
    (POW Transit Camp)
13/Lehr-Regiment Brandenburg 800
Feldpostamt zbV (m) 659
Feldpostamt zbV (m) 762
Feldpostamt zbV (m) Luftwaffe
Feldpostamt zbV (m) anstelle Armee-Briefstelle

This clearly shows the vast 'tail' of support required by a modern army in the field.

On the upgrading of the Korps to a Panzer-gruppe, the Deutsches Afrikakorps became a component part of the larger whole. Command of the Deutsches Afrikakorps passed to Generalleutnant Ludwig Crüwell until March 1942, when he was succeeded by Generalleutnant Walter Nehring. Nehring was wounded in action in August 1942 and evacuated, but returned in November to take command of German forces in Tunisia. These forces officially became known as XC Korps on 19 November. This short-lived command lasted only until 9 December when Hitler decided to upgrade the command structure in Tunisia and announced the formation of Panzer-Armeeoberkommando 5 under Generaloberst Jürgen von Arnim. XC Korps being absorbed into the new structure.

In December 1942 the Armeeoberkommando 5 order of battle was as follows:

Stab der Panzerarmee
10 Panzer Division
Division von Broich
20 Flak Division
I Batterie/Flak Regiment 54
II Batterie/Flak Regiment 54
Abwehrgruppe 210
Propaganda Zug Tunis
Armee Reserve
Division 'Imperiali'

By March 1943 it had expanded considerably, to include the following:

Stab der Panzerarmee
10 Panzer Division
21 Panzer Division
334 Infanterie Division
Division von Manteuffel
19 Flak Division
20 Flak Division
schwere Panzer Abteilung 501
Nachrichten Abteilung 190
Aufklärungs Abteilung 190
leichte Vermessungs und Kartenabteilung
Kampfgruppe Buhse
Kampfgruppe Schmid
Abschnitt Benigni

In February 1943 it was decided that the numbers of personnel and units in North Africa had expanded so much that a major command formation was necessary. On 23 February it was announced that Generalfeldmarschall Rommel was to take command of Heeresgruppe Afrika which would consist of both the 1 italienische Armee and Panzer-Armeeoberkommando 5. The Axis forces were now at last under a unified command, just under three months before they would unconditionally surrender.

In addition to the major commands listed above a considerable number of Kampfgruppen were formed, ranging from small units of only two or three companies to major forces of divisional strength or greater. These were usually formed from components of the major units already mentioned, for specific tasks such as local counterattacks, rearguard actions, etc. Because of the temporary nature of these formations they are not covered in this work.

Air and Sea Forces

Although the desert war was of course primarily a land battle, the Luftwaffe and Kriegsmarine played essential supporting rôles. The German Navy had no major warships based in North African ports. Its major functions in this area were coastal security and escort duties for supply convoys from Italy. Main naval bases in North Africa were located at Bizerta, Tripoli, Benghazi and Tobruk.

The Luftwaffe played a major part in the successes of Rommel's forces in North Africa. Amongst the first units to arrive were the Messerschmitt Bf110 twin-engined fighters of III/Zerstörergeschwader 26 and Messerschmitt Bf109s of I/Jagdgeschwader 27 and 7/Jagdgeschwader 26, with the Junkers Ju87 Stukas of II/Sturzkampfgeschwader 2.

Night fighter units also saw action in North Africa in defence against British bombing raids, both 1/Nachtjagdgeschwader 3 and 2/Nachtjagdgeschwader 2 serving in this theatre. Other Luftwaffe units which served at one time or another in support of

eneral KIRCHHEIM (Deutsches Afrikakorps)

Typical example of a senior officer's privately tailored tropical dress uniform in brown wool; Gen. Heinrich Kirchheim —awarded the Knight's Cross in May 1941, and at one point commander of the Italian 'Brescia' Division—wears the full set of hand-embroidered gold bullion insignia from his continental uniform.

Rommel's Afrikakorps included II/JG 27, and elements from JG77, JG2, JG26, JG53, ZG1, SG1, SG2 and KG26.

Although no Waffen-SS units served in North Africa, the Sicherheitsdienst (SD), the security arm of the SS, did have a base in Tunis, where they worked in close collaboration with the local police (and no doubt, the Geheime Feldpolizei) against subversives, black marketeers, etc. Photographs do exist of SS personnel wearing the 'Afrika' commemorative cufftitle, proving their service in North Africa.

Commanders of the German Forces in North Africa

Generalfeldmarschall Erwin Rommel
15 August 1941–9 September 1942
19 March 1942–22 September 1942
25 October 1942–23 February 1943
Generalleutnant Ludwig Crüwell
9 March 1942–19 March 1942
General Georg Stumme
22 September 1942–24 October 1942
Generalleutnant Wilhelm Ritter von Thoma
24 October 1942–25 October 1942
Generale di Armata Messe
23 February 1943–13 May 1943

Damaged and abandoned Panzer IIIs of 15 Panzer-Division. Possession of the field at the end of a battle made a great deal of difference—the enemy was denied the opportunity to recover and repair equipment, which became a total loss, while many of the victor's own could be put back into commission.

THE MAJOR FORMATIONS

5 leichte Division/21 Panzer Division

The first of the 'African' divisions, 5 leichte was specifically assembled for service in North Africa. It was constructed around cadre personnel from 3 Panzer Division, including Panzer Regiment 5. The first elements of the division arrived in North Africa on 14 February 1941, with its armour arriving by the end of the month. During the next few months the division took part in many major battles including the drive to Egypt and the attempt to take Tobruk. The division was strengthened by the addition of 104 Panzer Grenadier Regiment from 15 Panzer Division, and was retitled 21 Panzer Division from 1 October 1941.

The division took part in the defensive actions against the British 'Crusader' offensive in November

Rommel awarding the Iron Cross 2nd Class to DAK soldiers, 31 August 1942. Note turn-back cuffs of his privately tailored tunic; and Panzer collar patch skulls worn on the nearest soldier's lower lapels. As in so many photos, the field caps appear more bleached than the tunics. (Josef Charita)

1941, which virtually decimated the British 7th Armoured Brigade. Despite early successes, however, the German forces slowly disengaged, eventually pulling back to El Agheila. In early 1942 21 Panzer Division took part in Rommel's offensive leading to the fall of Benghazi on 29 January. Subsequently it acquitted itself well during the attack on the Gazala Line and the capture of Tobruk.

Finally checked by the British at El Alamein in July 1942, it was badly battered during the British 'Lightfoot' and 'Supercharge' operations in October and November 1942, being left with only a handful of tanks. During the subsequent retreat it served as rearguard for the Axis forces, enhancing its reputation by its tenacity and steadfastness during retreat.

By February 1943 the division had been strengthened considerably and had some 90 tanks. It took part in the battle for Sidi Bou Zid on 14/15 February and captured Sbeitla on 17 February. The division was part of Rommel's forces for the successful attack at Kasserine Pass before being halted at Sbiba. The remaining weeks of its life were spent in defensive actions before surrendering between 11 and 13 May.

Commanders

Generalmajor Johannes Streich
20 February–22 July 1941
Generalmajor Johann von Ravenstein
23 July–29 November 1941

Oberstleutnant Gustav-Georg Knabe
29 November–30 November 1941
Generalleutnant Karl Böttcher
30 November 1941–30 January 1942
Generalmajor Georg von Bismarck
30 January–31 August 1942
Oberst Carl-Hans Lungershausen
31 August–18 September 1942
Generalmajor Heinz von Randow
18 September–21 December 1942
Oberst Hans-Georg Hildebrandt
1 January–25 April 1943
Generalmajor Heinrich-Hermann von Hülsen
25 April–13 May 1943

Major units (Feb. 1941)
Panzer Regiment 5; I/Panzerjägerabteilung (mot) 33; Panzerjägerabteilung (mot) 39; Machinengewehr Bataillon (mot) 2; Machinengewehr Btl. (mot) 8; I/Artillerie Regt. (mot) 75; Luftwaffe Flak-Abteilung 605 & 606; Aufklärungs Abteilung (mot) 3.
(1942) Panzer Regt. 5; Panzerjäger Abteilung (mot) 39; Infanterie Regt. (mot) 104; Artillerie Regt. (mot) 155; Aufklärungs-Abteilung (mot) 3; divisional units numbered '200'.

10 Panzer Division

Formed in the summer of 1939, 10 Panzer Division played a minor part in the Polish Campaign before, in

1940, proving itself as part of Guderian's XIX Korps during the breakthrough at Sedan and the dash to the Channel coast. During the invasion of the Soviet Union, 10 Panzer Division took part in the attack on Minsk and Smolensk. It was heavily involved in the defensive actions against the 1941/42 Soviet winter offensive, successfully holding Rzhev against numerous enemy attacks.

Badly battered, the division was withdrawn to France for refitting, and took part in the occupation of the Vichy-controlled sector in November 1942 before being transferred to North Africa and immediately thrown into the battles for the Tunis bridgehead. Being recently refitted and at full strength, it proved invaluable. The division took part in the battle for Sidi Bou Zid split into Kampfgrup-

A well-known but interesting shot of Rommel with Generalmajor Ramcke, summer 1942. The paratroop commander wears the very loose-cut Luftwaffe tropical trousers with left thigh pocket; the shoulder straps and gold-bullion-on-grey breast eagle from his continental uniform are attached to the tropical field blouse. He wears the 'Hermann Meyer' cap; the cockade on the band is worn alone, without the traditional winged oakleaf wreath. (Josef Charita)

pen, and achieved considerable success. During the retreat in April/May 1943 the division served as a mobile reserve. Weakened in fierce fighting, the division was eventually pushed back into the hills north of Bizerte, surrendering on 9 May 1943. Among the units held on the division's order of battle was an assault regiment from the Luftwaffe's 'Hermann Göring' Division.

Commanders

Generalmajor Ferdinand Schaal
1939–2 August 1941
Generalleutnant Wolfgang Fischer
2 August 1941–1 February 1943
Generalmajor Fritz Freiherr von Broich
1 February–12 May 1943

Major units (Jan. 1943)

Panzer Regiment 7; Panzerjäger Abteilung (mot) 90; Infanterie Regts. (mot) 69 & 86; Sturmregiment 'Hermann Göring'; Inf. Btl. (mot) A4; Artillerie-Regt. (mot) 90; Flak Gruppe Böhmer (Luftwaffe); variously numbered divisional units.

15 Panzer Division

This veteran division was originally formed in April 1936 as 33 Infanterie Division based in Kaiserslautern, composed of 104, 110 and 115 Infanterie Regiments. The division saw action during the fall of France before being reformed as a Panzer Division in the autumn of 1940.

The division arrived in North Africa in April 1941, just too late to take part in Rommel's capture of Benghazi. By the end of June, however, it was in action in defensive moves against the British 'Brevity' and 'Battleaxe' operations around Tobruk. In November 1941 the British launched Operation 'Crusader' and 15 Panzer Division found itself in the thick of the fighting. It was reduced to a handful of operational tanks and had to be withdrawn for refitting.

The division was reinforced with shipments of fresh armour from Europe, and in January 1942 15 Panzer went on to the offensive during Rommel's successful attempt to take Benghazi; in May it took part in the battles on the Gazala Line. Having taken Bir Hacheim, Rommel once more unleashed his forces on Tobruk, and within five days the port had

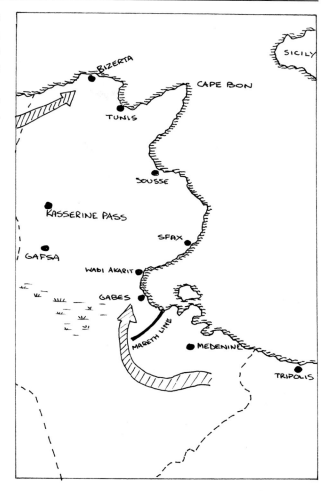

The end in Africa: British forces from Tripolitania in the south-east, and Anglo-American and French forces from Algeria in the west, forced the Panzerarmee slowly into the north-east of Tunisia, where they were eventually compelled to surrender in May 1943. Very few escaped to Sicily, and the loss of a quarter of a million men was as serious a blow to the Axis as Stalingrad.

fallen. There was to be no rest for the men of 15 Panzer, however, as Rommel's forces pursued the retreating British over the border into Egypt. By 1 July 15 Panzer was involved in the first battle of El Alamein. This first attack, on well-prepared British positions, was unsuccessful, as were subsequent attacks on Alam Halfa on 30 August and 1 September. On 2 September, Rommel abandoned his attack.

On 23 October Montgomery commenced his counter-offensive, and in the battles which followed 15 Panzer Division was decimated. By early November Panzer Regiment 8 had lost all of its tanks as well

German officer prisoners wearing a variety of uniform items. Note the all-brown tropical greatcoat; sand-painted helmets both with and without the decal left visible; continental breast eagle and collar patches; and use of a sweater under the tunic. (IWM)

Oberst Hans-Carl Freiherr von Esebeck
15 April–25 July 1941
Generalmajor Walter Neumann-Silkow
25 July–6 December 1941
Oberst Erwin Menny
6 December–8 December 1941
Generalleutnant Gustav von Vaerst
9 December 1941–26 May 1942
Oberst Eduard Craseman
26 May–8 July 1942
Generalleutnant Gustav von Vaerst
8 July–31 August 1942
Generalmajor Heinz von Randow
1 September–17 September 1942
Generalleutnant Gustav von Vaerst
17 September–12 December 1942
Oberst Willibald Boroweitz
12 December 1942–13 May 1943

Major units (April 1942)

Panzer Regiment 8; Panzerjäger Abteilung (mot) 33; Infanterie Regt. (mot) 115; Artillerie Regt. (mot) 33; Aufklärungs-Abteilung (mot) 33; divisional units numbered '33'.

90 leichte Afrika Division

This division was formed in August 1941 in Libya as 'Afrika Division zbV' from a number of existing units already serving in Africa, and included 155, 200 and 361 Motorised Infantry Regiments. Its first combat followed in the battle for Tobruk on 21 November 1941 where it acquitted itself well. One week later its title was changed to 90 leichte Afrika Division.

'90th Light' was involved in the retreat from Cyrenaica and the recapture of Benghazi in January 1942. It was also committed to the attack on the Gazala Line from 26 May to 14 June and the sieges of Got el Ualeb and Bir Hacheim. On 29 June the British fortress of Mersa Matruh fell to a German force which included 90 leichte Division. Constant action, however, saw the division reduced to some 1,600 men by the end of June. Nevertheless, it fought again during the first assault on El Alamein.

In October 1942, when Montgomery launched his long-awaited offensive, the division was holding the northernmost coastal sector of the German line. It suffered dreadful losses, as indeed did most of the German forces, losing, on average, at least half their

as its regimental commander. Forced to retreat into Tunisia, it went into reserve under 1 italiensiche Armee.

The division, with much of its armoured strength replenished, went on to the offensive at Medenine on 6 March 1943 and gained initial success, but British superiority in numbers soon pushed the Germans back again, with the loss of 24 of the division's precious tanks. On 22 March the division, still part of the German reserves, was again committed to action in a counterattack against the British at Wadi Zigaou, and with some success. When, on 27 March, a strong Allied force broke through the German lines at El Hauma 15 Panzer Division was thrown into the line to halt them. By now, however, it could field only ten serviceable Panzers, and was pushed back relentlessly. By early May the Division was cut off in a pocket alongside Division von Manteuffel and 10 Panzer Division. On 9 May, 15 Panzer Division surrendered to the British.

Commanders
Generalmajor Heinrich von Prittwitz
22 March–10 April 1941

strength. For the last few months of the desert war, the remnants of the division acted as Rommel's rearguard, constantly involved in defensive actions. By early April 1943 its strength was estimated at 5,700 men. On 12 May it finally surrendered north of Enfidaville.

Commanders

Generalmajor Max Sümmerman
17 July–10 December 1941
Oberst Johann Mickl
11 December–27 December 1941
Generalmajor Richard Veith
28 December 1941–28 April 1942
Generalmajor Ulrich Kleeman
29 April–14 June 1942
Oberst Werner Marcks
14 June–18 June 1942
Oberst Erwin Menny
18 June–19 June 1942
Oberst Werner Marcks
19 June–21 June 1942
Generalmajor Ulrich Kleeman
21 June–8 September 1942
Generalmajor Bernhard Hermann Ramcke
8 September–17 September 1942
Oberst Hermann Schulte-Heuthaus
17 September–22 September 1942
Generalleutnant Theodor Graf von Sponek
22 September /Ç·¿–12 May 1943

Major units (late 1942)

Infanterie Regiment (mot) 155; Inf. Regt. (mot) 200 (formed March 1942 from elements IRs 155 & 347); Inf. Regt. Afrika 361 (partly formed from French Foreign Legion veterans); Panzergrenadier Regt. (mot) Afrika (previously 'Sonderverband 288'); Dec. 1942, Kolbeck-BH. (transport & flak personnel plus released IR 361 prisoners); Panzerjäger Abteilung (mot) 190; Artillerie Regt. (mot) 190; Aufklärungs Abt. (mot) 580; variously numbered divisional units.

164 leichte Afrika Division

This division was raised in the winter of 1939/40 in Königsbrück as 164 Infanterie Lehr Division,

DAK soldier posing in full tropical uniform of early manufacture, with pleated pockets under scalloped flaps.

around 382, 433 and 440 Infanterie Regiments. It did not take part in the campaign in the West but was used in the Balkans, being stationed on occupation duties in Greece for a year before being moved to Crete. In early July 1942 the division was moved to North Africa and redesignated 164 leichte Afrika Division. It arrived in the nick of time. 382 Infanterie Regiment arrived at the Panzerarmee Afrika HQ just as its defenders were about to be overrun.

The division's first major action was at the end of August when it took part in a raid against Australian forces at El Alamein. After the British offensive of October 1942 the division fought in the rearguard, divisional units being dispersed and attached to armoured formations as support troops.

The division had a spell out of the line for rest and refit until early December when it was tasked to prepare defensive positions at Buerat. At around this time the division became fully motorised. In March 1943 the British launched a major attack on the Mareth Line, New Zealand infantry overrunning some of the division's units, and 164 leichte was forced to withdraw. By April the last of the division's vehicles had been lost and 164 leichte was once again reduced to footslogging infantry. By the time it finally surrendered on 13 May it had been reduced to some 5,000 men.

Commanders
Oberst Carl-Hans Lungershausen
August 1942–31 August 1942
Oberst Hermann-Hans Hecker
31 August–18 September 1942
Oberst Carl-Hans Lungershausen
9 September–end November 1942
Oberst Siegfried Westphal
6 December–30 December 1942
Generalmajor Kurt Freiherr von Liebenstein
1 January–16 January 1943
Oberst Becker
16 January–17 February 1943
Generalmajor Fritz Krause
17 February–13 March 1943
Generalmajor Kurt Freiherr von Liebenstein
13 March–13 May 1943

Major units
Panzergrenadier Regts. (mot) 125, 382, 433; Artillerie Regt. (mot) 220; Flak-Abteilung (mot) 609; Aufklärungs Abteilung (mot) 220; divisional units numbered '220'.

334 Infanterie Division
This division was raised in the autumn of 1942, with its home base in Wehrkreis XIII, the Nuremberg area. Shortly after working up the division's first elements were sent to North Africa in December 1942. It was allocated to Panzer Armee-Oberkommando 5 and was assigned to cover the sector of the front between Division von Broich and 10 Panzer Division. Whilst the greater part of the division was held in reserve, Infanterie Regiment 754 was temporarily allocated to 10 Panzer Division and took part in the battles over the Christmas period of 1942. Infanterie Regiment 755 arrived in North Africa in early January 1943, and by the middle of the

Haggling in a native bazaar, two junior NCOs; the original colour print shows the left hand man to wear infantry white piping on his shoulder straps, his mate armour pink piping. The left hand cap and tunic are of warmer brown shades of olive than the right hand uniform, which is distinctly greener. (Josef Charita)

month the division was at full strength, taking part in Gen. von Arnim's drive towards Bou Arada. The division was involved in fierce and continuous combat until, by the start of March, the Korpsgruppe to which it was attached had only six tanks left.

In late April 334 Infanterie Division provided 'Gruppe Audorff', which was used in the attack on the heights of Medjez el Bab, being halted after some initial successes. The inevitable British counterattack was aimed at the German positions around Hill 296 (Longstop Hill). Infanterie Regiment 756 held the position against several British attacks over four days of intense combat but was eventually pushed back.

As the campaign in North Africa moved towards its conclusion in May 1943 the division was pulled out of the line and moved to an area north of Medjerda. Lack of fuel led to the inevitable loss of mobility, and the division became cut off and surrounded by enemy forces. After a futile attempt to break out the division finally surrendered to the British on 8 May between Mateur and Terbourba. The division was reformed in France in late summer 1943, serving for the remainder of the war on the Eastern Front.

Commanders
Oberst Friedrich Weber
13 November 1942–15 April 1943
Generalmajor Fritz Krause
15 April–8 May 1943

Major units (Nov. 1942)
Infanterie Regts. (mot) 754, 755; Gebirgs Inf. Regt. (mot) 756; Panzerjäger Abteilung (mot) 334; Artillerie Regt. (mot) 334; divisional units numbered '334'.

999 leichte Afrika Division
Formed late in 1942 near Antwerp, this division was one of the German Army's penal units. The bulk of the personnel comprised both minor political offenders and criminals, such as black marketeers, for whom military service had been authorised as a form of rehabilitation. Originally of brigade strength, it was upgraded to a division in March 1943. Its officers and NCOs were hand-picked, reliable and experienced soldiers. In March 1943 two of its regiments,

961 and 962 Rifle Regiments, were moved to North Africa. The divisional commander, Generalmajor Kurt Thomas, was reported missing in action when his plane was shot down on his way to the North African front. Because of this there was to be no time for a formalised divisional HQ element to be formed during the short period the unit served in North Africa. (Thomas was reportedly promoted to Generalleutnant in October 1943 and killed in action on the Eastern Front, so apparently survived the shooting down of his plane.)

Shortly after its arrival in Africa, Schützen-Regiment (mot) 961 was attached to 'Kampfgruppe Fullreide' and took part in the defensive actions following the British offensive in the Fondouk area on 7/8 April. Schützen Regiment (mot) 962 took part in the defence of 'Longstop Hill' during the middle of April. For the next few weeks the division's elements in North Africa fought in numerous defensive actions, before surrendering on 13 May 1943. In view of its short period of service in North Africa, and the 'criminal' nature of many of its personnel, the division performed well. Those elements not sent to North Africa were posted to Greece.

Commanders
Generalleutnant Kurt Thomas
23 December 1942–1 April 1943
Oberst Ernst-Günther Baade
2 April–13 May 1943

Major units (Jan. 1943)
Afrika Schützen-Regts. (mot) 961, 962; divisional units numbered '999'.

Division von Broich/von Manteuffel
In early November 1942 'Stab Lederer' was formed to control all German units in Tunisia. Changed a few days later to 'Stab Stolz', it was once again renamed on 18 November 'Division von Broich'. This formation included such diverse forces as a Fallschirmjäger Regiment and an Italian Bersaglieri Regiment as well as infantry and artillery troops. On 26 November the division took part in the first clash between German and US armour in World War Two.

In December 1942 Panzer Armee-Oberkommando 5 was formed and Division von

Broich came under its control, being allocated to the northern sector of the Tunisian front. On 7 February 1943 Generalmajor der Panzertruppe Hasso von Manteuffel took command of the division when von Broich was posted to take command of 10 Panzer Division, whose commander had been killed in action. The division's title was altered to 'Division von Manteuffel' at this time.

This famous Panzer general commanded the division during the German offensive from 26 February to 15 March 1943, when it advanced almost to Djebel Aboud before heavy losses halted its progress. On 31 March command passed to Generalleutnant Bülowius; the division remained on the northern sector of the front during the final battles before surrendering on 9 May 1943.

Commanders
Oberst Fritz Freiherr von Broich
           18 November 1942–5 February 1943
Generalmajor Hasso von Manteuffel
           7 February–31 March 1943
Generalleutnant Bülowius
           31 March–9 May 1943

Major units (March 1943)
Fallschirmjäger Regt. (mot) 'Barenthin' (Luftwaffe); Panzergrenadier Regt. (mot) 160; Bersaglieri Regt. (mot) 10 (Italian); IV/Afrika Artillerie Regt. (mot) 2; variously numbered Army and Luftwaffe divisional units.

Division 'Hermann Göring'

This formidable formation evolved from Polizei-abteilung zbV Wecke, established in February 1933 by Hermann Göring in his capacity as Prussian Minister of the Interior. Initially a Police unit used against enemies of the state such as Communists, by September 1935 it had been reformed as a Landes-polizei Gruppe, and then as a Regiment, but still under Police control. On 24 September 1935, however, Göring had the unit transferred en bloc to the Luftwaffe as 'Regiment Hermann Göring', and supplied cadre personnel for the Luftwaffe's first Fallschirmjäger units.

Accorded élite status from the start, the unit had very strict recruitment standards; and like its counterparts—the 'Leibstandarte' in the SS and 'Grossdeutschland' in the Army—it had a high profile in pre-war years, appearing at parades and ceremonial events and boasting a fine regimental band. The unit took part in the Austrian Anschluss and the occupation of the Sudetenland.

A small element took part in the Polish campaign, and 'Hermann Göring' sub-units were also involved in Norway; the regiment also acquitted itself well during the fall of France. Committed to the Balkan campaign, the regiment served in Rumania before taking part in Operation 'Barbarossa', the invasion of the Soviet Union. It distinguished itself at Radzrechow, Dubno, Kiev and Bryansk. In March 1942 the regiment was expanded to brigade status; in October 1942 it was enlarged yet again, to divisional strength. It was during this period of expansion that the division was ordered to Italy; and in late 1943 elements were sent to North Africa. Two battalions of the division's Jäger Regiment were first into action in March 1943, and saw combat while attached to 10. Panzer-Division. Units arriving piecemeal in North Africa came under control of the advance party 'Vorkommando Hermann Göring' under Oberst Schmid (promoted Generalmajor on 1 March) and were known as 'Kampfgruppe Schmid'.

By mid-February 1943 Kampfgruppe Schmid was located on the southern sector of the Tunisian front. 'Hermann Göring' units sent to North Africa were often reinforced in combat by piecemeal elements of other units committed as they arrived. Formed units included: I/Panzer Regiment 'HG'; I & III/Grenadier-Regt. 'HG'; I & III/Jäger Regt. 'HG'; I & II/Flak Regt. 'HG'; and various reconnaissance elements.

These units fought with distinction until forced to surrender on 12 May, a small number of personnel managing to escape by air to Sicily. The formation was very rapidly rebuilt in southern France and Italy as a Panzer Division. (See Osprey Vanguard 4, *Fallschirm-panzerdivision 'Hermann Göring'*.)

Fallschirmjäger Brigade Ramcke
Originally intended for the invasion of Malta, this Luftwaffe paratroop formation was sent to Africa in response to Rommel's call for reinforcements in summer 1942, being flown in during August. Commanded by Generalmajor Bernhardt Ramcke, it comprised four rifle battalions, an artillery battalion,

an anti-tank and a pioneer company. The unit, airlifted from Europe, had no transport, and was driven directly to the front by a Flak unit. It took up positions between the Italian 'Bologna' and 'Brescia' Divisions facing the southern sector of the El Alamein line. After bitter resistance to the British offensive in late October the brigade was forced to withdraw from the collapsing front of the Italian X Corps; it had already been written off as destroyed by Rommel's staff. In fact some 600 men of the brigade carried out an epic 200-mile retreat across open desert dominated by the enemy, capturing British transport and supplies on the way, and rejoining the German forces near Fuka. The brigade later fought with distinction in Tunisia. (See also Osprey Men-at-Arms 139, *German Airborne Troops 1939–45*.)

Special Units:
Infanterie Lehr Regiment zbV Brandenburg

This famous unit was probably the nearest thing the Wehrmacht fielded to Britain's SAS. It carried out commando-type raids behind enemy lines, its soldiers being trained in sabotage techniques and often speaking several languages. Brandenburgers often operated in enemy uniforms, and recorded several ingenious successes in these operations on all fronts.

The first use of the Brandenburgers in North Africa was in June 1941 when they were used for deep reconnaissance tasks. A special Tropical Company was formed (Tropen Kompanie Brandenburg) under Oberleutnant Fritz von Koenen; half of this 300-strong unit reached Africa in October, and was used in late 1941 in sabotage missions behind enemy lines. It is known that German commando-type raids reached almost as far as Cairo, causing considerable damage and alarm to the British.

In December 1942, a small glider-borne force from I/Regt. 4 Brandenburg destroyed the rail bridge at Sidi bou Baker in Tunisia and escaped unscathed. Another party was captured north of Kasserine.

Expanded to battalion strength and entitled Abteilung von Koenen in January 1943 the Brandenburg element based in North Africa took part in the last German attack of the desert war when it attacked US positions near Sidi bou Zid on 14 February. The Americans were thrown back, losing nearly 30 tanks, 23 guns, 100 vehicles and over 700 prisoners. When the Deutsches Afrikakorps surrendered in May 1943

Fine studio pose by a young DAK soldier in regulation uniform, his peaked field cap bearing the soutache of Waffenfarbe (in fact, the centrally sewn lace known as 'Russia braid') round the national cockade. Note loop-and-button fastening for the shoulder straps; and unobtrusive appearance of the 'all ranks' collar Litzen in grey-blue on tan.

the Brandenburgers were not to be caught; they commandeered various boats and escaped over the Mediterranean to southern Italy. The unit later saw action against partisans in the Balkans, where Von Koenen was killed in August 1944.

Sonderverband 288

In mid-1941 a Brandenburg company designated Sonderverband 287 was formed at Potsdam-Ruinenberg, and later trained in tropical warfare in southern Greece. A sister company, Sonderverband 288, was formed and trained soon afterwards, and subsequently expanded and designated an independent motorised Kampfgruppe. Both units were origin-

Excellent portrait study of a Ritterkreuzträger, Stabsfeldwebel Wilhelm Wendt; the senior warrant officer of 5 Kompanie, Panzer-Regiment 5, 21 Panzer-Division, he was awarded the Knight's Cross on 30 June 1941. The field cap is so bleached as to appear white, contrasting with the dark olive tunic. The 'pips' on the shoulder straps, and the collar Litzen, both appear unusually light, and may have been 'worked on' for this, obviously his best walking-out dress. Of particular interest are the Spanish Cross on his right pocket, and the Condor Legion Panzer Badge—a rare award—next to the conventional Panzer Battle Badge on his left pocket. (Josef Charita)

companies capable of independent operations. Two battalions and all officers were selected from colonial Germans from the Middle East and former African colonies; the third was made up of Arabs.

Attached to 90 leichte Afrika Division, Sonderverband 288 apparently fought with some distinction in the first six months of 1942. On 6 August a Panzerarmee Stab order reorganised and redesignated the unit as Panzergrenadier Regiment (mot) Afrika, though the actual redesignation did not take effect until 31 October. The unit continued to fight effectively, seeing action at Bir Hacheim, Tobruk, and in the retreat into Tunisia.

'Free Arabian Corps'

After the failure of the Iraqi rising in summer 1941 numbers of Arab sympathisers were shipped out of the Middle East by the Germans and gathered at Cape Sunion, near Athens, as Sonderstab Felmy. In January 1942 the group, at company strength, was retitled Deutsche-Arabische Lehr Abteilung; the DAL was sometimes colloquially called the 'Free Arabian Corps', and received German Army tropical uniforms with the right sleeve patch illustrated (see Plates A, K). A second company was raised in summer 1942, mainly from French North African volunteers; and about 600 DAL personnel later saw active service in North Africa, though little combat—morale apparently slumped after the death of the CO, Oberst Meyer-Ricko. A third company raised in Greece in spring 1943 remained there on security duties.

UNIFORMS AND INSIGNIA

Unlike the unfortunate Wehrmacht soldiers on the Eastern Front who suffered the horrors of the Russian winter of 1941/42 in clothing suitable only for moderate climates, the soldiers of the Afrikakorps were well equipped. As soon as German involvement in the Mediterranean area and Middle East began to seem likely the Tropical Institute of Hamburg University was commissioned to develop a range of tropical uniforms, and by late 1940 large stocks were

ally intended to exploit the Rachid Ali uprising against the British in Iraq, and to make their way via Iraq into British-occupied Palestine and Egypt, perhaps even reaching the Suez Canal zone. The failure of the Iraqi uprising led to Sonderverband 287 being retained in Greece and later sent to Russia on anti-partisan duties; 288 was shipped directly to North Africa, commanded by Oberst Menton. It was organised in three small battalions totalling 12

already available. The basic range of Army tropical clothing included the following:

Headgear

The Pith Helmet

This was a conventional sun helmet made from compressed cork, and covered with segments of olive green canvas cloth. The interior of the helmet was lined with red cloth and the underside of the rim with green cloth. It featured leather binding to the edge of the rim, a leather sweatband and a leather chinstrap. Insignia, matching that on the steel helmet, consisted of two light metal alloy shields, one featuring the national eagle and swastika emblem in silver on black, and the other the national colours of red, silver and black in slanting stripes. These were attached to the helmet by three prongs on the reverse.

The helmet was widely issued, but was not particularly popular with the troops, who almost invariably discarded it in favour of the field cap. It was, however, often worn behind the front lines for semi-formal occasions, parades, etc. A second version of the pith helmet was produced in compressed felt of a distinct brownish hue from late 1942 onwards. It is not thought that these saw issue in North Africa, but they were used in other parts of the Mediterranean theatre.

The Sidecap

Based on the continental M38 field cap, this was a peakless sidecap made in olive cloth lined with red cotton. Unlike those of the peaked field cap, the side flaps were not false and could be folded down. Ventilation was by a single metal grommet on each side of the crown. It was not particularly widely used, but was popular with the crews of armoured vehicles, where the long peak of the field cap could be awkward. Early examples featured a Waffenfarbe chevron over the cockade in the same manner as the peaked field cap.

The Peaked Field Cap

The most popular piece of headgear worn by the Afrikakorps was the ubiquitous peaked field cap. This was closely styled on the peaked 'ski-cap' or Bergmütze of the Mountain Troops. It was manufactured from light olive canvas material, and featured a long peak giving excellent protection to the eyes. Unlike the mountain cap, the flaps on the tropical

Major Dr. Heinrich Drewes, CO of Kradschutzen-Bataillon 10, was decorated with the Knight's Cross on 24 April 1943, just before the end in Tunisia. Note hand-embroidered bullion collar patches; and continental breast eagle on dark green backing, though unusually it seems to be machine-woven in 'other ranks'' style rather than embroidered. The cap is an 'other ranks'' model too, 'up-graded' by the addition of twisted silver cord to the crown seam and front scallop—issue officers' caps had woven aluminium piping, not twisted cord.

model were false. The cap had two metal grommets each side of the crown for ventilation, and was lined in red cotton.

Both the sidecap and the peaked field cap were distinguished by woven aluminium braid piping to the crown seam and front 'scallop' on officers' versions; occasionally, however, other ranks' versions were converted by adding twisted cord piping to the crown and scallop.

Insignia for all ranks consisted of a woven silk pale-blue-on-tan eagle and swastika over a silk cockade in the black/white/red national colours woven on to a tan backing. Prior to July 1942 an inverted chevron of Waffenfarbe colour piping was worn over the cockade to indicate the branch of service.

The olive colour of the cap quickly faded in the strong desert sun. Many soldiers deliberately bleached their headgear as a faded cap was the prestigious mark of the veteran campaigner, and a dark cap the mark of the 'new boy'.

(This cap has become the single most popular item of Afrikakorps uniform among collectors, just as it was the single most recognisable 'symbol' of the desert soldier—indeed, it was often the only piece of uniform dress worn to show the nationality of its wearer. Originals of this cap are now extremely expensive, and they are being widely reproduced. Some copies made in Germany are highly accurate and difficult to detect.)

Uniform garments
The Field Blouse
The tropical field blouse was manufactured in olive lightweight cotton in open-neck style with four pleated patch pockets, two at the breast and two on the skirt, with buttoned flaps. The blouse was fastened at the front by five olive green-painted metal buttons. Buttons on the tropical field blouse were removable, being held in place by split rings in the blouse interior. The blouse had a field dressing pocket on the right hand interior flap at the base, and had two belt hook retaining straps. The cuffs were adjustable, with button fastening.

Insignia included standardised collar patches for all ranks—pale blue-grey Litzen on a tan backing—and a machine woven silk breast eagle in pale blue on

A group of Luftwaffe aircrew, wearing a variety of flying overalls and a mixture of blue-grey and tropical field caps, enjoy a meal on a North African airstrip in February 1942. (Josef Charita)

tan, also common to all ranks. Shoulder straps for NCOs and other ranks were cut from the same material as the blouse and piped in the appropriate Waffenfarbe around the edge. NCOs had the tunic collar and the shoulder straps trimmed in NCO Tresse lace, the tropical-type lace being in a copper-brown colour rather than silver as on continental uniforms.

From late 1942 the tropical field blouse lost the pleats to the pockets, and shortly afterwards the scalloped edges of the pocket flaps were omitted, flaps being square cut subsequently.

Officers often elected to show their status by the use of the bullion hand-embroidered collar patches and breast eagle from their continental tunics instead of the basic tropical issue items. The removable pattern shoulder straps from officers' field grey continental tunics were standard wear on the tropical field blouse. General officers likewise often elected to wear all the insignia on the tropical field blouse in the standard form from their field grey dress. Senior officers occasionally had tailor-made tunics in tropical pattern, but cut from finer quality cloth than the issue olive green cotton.

The Tropical Shirt

A tropical shirt was issued in lightweight olive cotton; it was of the 'pullover' style with a four-button front, long tails, and two pleated patch breast pockets. It was often worn in lieu of the field blouse, with both breast eagle and shoulder straps added. A cotton tie of the same colour was issued with the shirt, but rarely worn.

Trousers

Long-legged olive cotton trousers were produced, featuring a concealed integral cloth waist belt, two slash side pockets, a hip pocket and a front fob pocket. The fly front was button-fastened. It was a popular fashion to sew a drawstring into the cuff of the leg to allow the trousers to be neatly 'bloused' where the trouser leg entered the boot. *Breeches* in similar material were also produced, as were *shorts*.

Trousers were popularly worn with the laced canvas and leather *ankle boot* (the upper part and the ankle of the boot being canvas), while the breeches were usually worn with the alternative issue *high leg lace-up boot*, also in canvas and leather. In theory, at least, shorts were not permitted in the front line.

A young Luftwaffe private in the pale tan tropical uniform. The breast eagle is machine-embroidered in grey cotton on a tan twill base, and was normally worn by all ranks. Collar patches were not worn on the tropical tunic. (Paul Anderson)

The tropical Fliegermütze, in pale golden-tan cotton and usually lined in bright red; the light grey eagle and swastika are machine-embroidered on a tan base; the black/white/red national cockade, unlike the Army equivalent, is a raised boss.

A fine study of two 'Hermann Meyer' caps being worn without the button-on neck flap, by personnel of the 'Hermann Göring' units rushed to Tunisia—note cufftitle just visible on right sleeve of Unteroffizier, left. This NCO wears full machine-woven insignia on his cap (and, unusually, tropical Tresse braid round his upper collar, although no patches were worn). His comrade has a machine-embroidered eagle and swastika sewn to the cap crown, and an unsupported cockade on the band. (Herbert E. Kail)

A mixture of Kriegsmarine tropical dress, more practical than elegant. The officer at left wears the tropical peaked field cap, shirt with added rank shoulder straps, shorts, and ankle boots. The officer in the centre wears shirt and shorts, with pin-on gilt metal breast eagle, and white-topped summer Schirmmütze; he seems to wear long socks and sandals. The officer on the right has the gold-piped dark blue naval officer's boarding cap, shirt, shorts, and laced shoes. (Josef Charita)

Uniform insignia: see text for captions

2

3

4

1

5a

5b

7a

7b

7c

7d

8

9

بلاد العرب الحرة

FREIES ARABIEN

VOLSTAD 91

6

A

Uniform insignia: see text for captions

B

Vehicle insignia: see text for captions

1

2

3

4

5

6

7

8

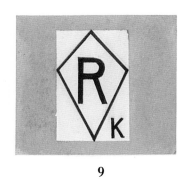

9

10

11

12

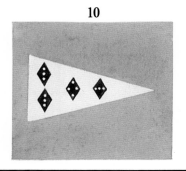

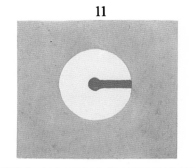

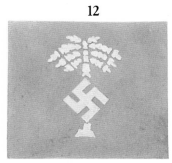

C

1: Obergefreiter, Infantry
2: Unteroffizier, Panzer troops
3: Feldwebel, Panzer troops

D

1: Major, Aufklärungs – Abteilung 33
2: Oberstleutnant, Infantry
3: Generalmajor

VOLSTAD 91

E

1: Oberfeldwebel, Pioneers
2: Unteroffizier, Pioneers
3: Obergefreiter, Artillery

F

1: Leutnant, Luftwaffe Flakartillerie
2: Hauptmann fighter pilot, Luftwaffe Fliegertruppe
3: Oberstleutnant, Luftwaffe Fliegertruppe

G

1: Jäger, Fallschirmjäger–Brigade Ramcke, 1942
2: Oberfeldwebel, Panzer Regiment 'Hermann Göring', 1943
3: Leutnant, Jäger Regiment 'Hermann Göring', 1943

H

1: Bootsmann, Kriegsmarine, shore duty
2: Kapitänleutnant, Kriegsmarine
3: Stabsteuermann, Kriegsmarine

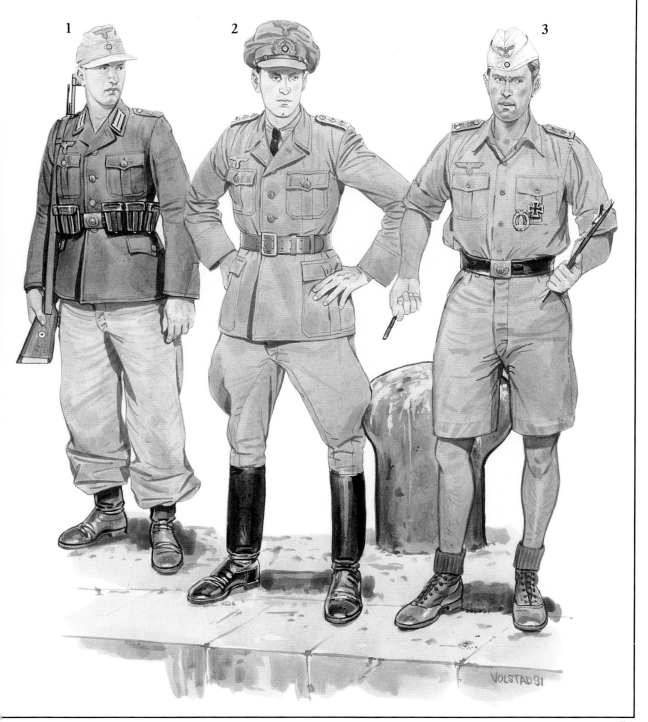

I

1: Oberfeldwebel, Sonderverband 288
2: Stabsfeldwebel, Feldgendarmerie
3: Sonderführer

J

1: Freiwilliger, Deutsche-Arabische Lehr-Abteilung
2: Army Protestant chaplain
3: SS-Untersturmführer, Einsatzkommando Tunis

K

1: Nurse, German Red Cross
2: Driver, 4th Motor Transport Regiment, NSKK
3: TN-Vormann, Technisches Nothilfe

L

A formal parade of Kriegsmarine personnel; tropical tunics, shirts and slacks are worn with the blue (or white-topped) headgear from continental uniform. The use of tropical breeches and jackboots (by the officer at centre) was rare in the navy. (Josef Charita)

The Greatcoat

Styled closely on the field grey continental greatcoat, the tropical version was made in darkish brown woollen cloth; it was double-breasted, with two rows of six olive-painted buttons, and featured an integral half-belt at the back. Unlike the continental version, which had a contrasting dark green-faced collar, the tropical greatcoat was cut all in the same material and colour.

The Motorcycle Coat

A tropical version of the motorcyclist's rubberised coat was manufactured in a similar olive colour to the tropical field blouse. Double-breasted, the coat featured two large side pockets and an angled document pocket in the chest. The coat could be fastened between the legs to make it less cumbersome when riding a motorcycle.

Luftwaffe Tropical Uniforms

The first Luftwaffe personnel to reach North Africa wore the standard Army tropical uniform, to which they attached their Luftwaffe collar patches. In late 1941, however, the Luftwaffe's own tropical clothing began to appear.

Headgear

The Pith Helmet

The Luftwaffe's version of the pith helmet was identical in basic construction to that of the Army; it differed in that it was covered in tan-coloured canvas, and in place of the eagle and swastika shield emblem it featured a 'flying' Luftwaffe eagle and swastika. This 'flew' in the same direction (i.e. right to left) as the Luftwaffe emblem on the steel helmet, the opposite to that on the cap and breast insignia.

The Sidecap

The Luftwaffe's tropical sidecap was identical in cut to that for the blue-grey continental uniform, lacking the scalloped flap of its Army counterpart. It was made in lightweight tan-coloured cotton and normally lined in bright red cotton (some tan-lined examples were also made). The eagle and swastika emblem on the crown was in light grey machine embroidery on tan backing, above a raised boss cockade in national colours. Officers were issued with a cap distinguished by silver cord piping to the flap, but generally with other ranks' insignia.

The Peaked Field Cap

A tropical field cap, similar to that of the Army but in tan rather than olive cloth, was produced, but does not appear to have been widespread official issue. Some had two-button front fastening on functional, rather than imitation flaps. Numerous variants were produced. Insignia were normally as those on the sidecap.

The Tropical Peaked Cap

This unique cap, which saw only limited wear, was basically similar in design to the standard officer's Schirmmütze peaked cap, but with all parts, including the large stiffened peak, made in tan cloth. No Waffenfarbe piping, as commonly found on other ranks' peaked caps, was applied, nor was silver cord piping for officers. (Some officers, however, did elect to wear the double silver bullion chin cords from the continental Schirmmütze on the tropical model.) The cap was lined in red cotton; and featured button fastenings on the lower edge of the band at the side and rear, to which a cloth protective neck flap could be attached. The standard chinstrap, as issued, was in leather and could be either natural leather colour or darkened to a dark brown, black or dark blue colour.

Insignia on this cap were based on those for the standard peaked cap, i.e. a flying eagle on the front of the crown, over a winged oakleaf wreath and cockade on the band. The insignia could be either machine woven or machine embroidered in light grey thread on tan. Occasionally, the cap could be seen with only the cockade worn on the band.

This cap was often jokingly referred to as the 'Hermann Meyer' cap, a reference to a boast made by the Luftwaffe's commander-in-chief Hermann Göring that if a single enemy bomber managed to attack the Reich, his name would be Meyer.

The Tropical Field Blouse

The Luftwaffe's tropical field blouse differed from that of the Army in two principal respects. Firstly, it was in the typical golden tan colour of the Luftwaffe rather than the Army's olive green; and secondly, it was designed to allow it to be fastened at the collar. Minor differences included the use of pleated breast pockets, but plain skirt pockets.

The blouse was worn without collar patches. Officers wore the shoulder straps from their continental service dress tunic. The breast eagle was in grey thread on tan for all ranks, though once again officers occasionally had hand-embroidered silver wire badges on tan backing made up for their tunics.

The Tropical Shirt

Similar to that of the Army, the Luftwaffe tropical shirt was of the pullover style, with two breast pockets. It was, however, made in golden tan cotton, and was issued with a breast eagle already attached. Shoulder straps were worn.

The Trousers

Luftwaffe trousers were similar to those of the Army but much more loosely fitting with very baggy legs. They featured ankle straps to blouse the legs, and a single large pocket on the front of the left thigh.

Full naval tropical dress, including the Kriegsmarine version of the peaked field cap, worn at an award ceremony in 1943. Note false turn-back cuffs of the officer's tropical blouse. (Josef Charita)

Besitzurkunde
Ich verleihe dem

Oberleutnant

Gerhard Kurtz

das
Ärmelband
~ Afrika ~

Hauptquartier des O.B.S., den 7.4.1943   Der Oberbefehlshaber Süd

Keßelring
Generalfeldmarschall

F. d. R.
Major

Besitzurkunde
Dem

wurde die
Erinnerungsmedaille
für den
italienisch-deutschen
Feldzug in Afrika
verliehen

Afrika, den .... 194..

Dunstsiegel

Unterschrift

Award document for 'Afrika' campaign cuffband—the more elaborate of two typical patterns, with the palm tree motif. It is unusual among German award certificates in giving only name and rank, not the recipient's unit. (Paul Anderson)

Unissued certificate for the Italo-German campaign medal, bearing the Arco de Fellini, also the central motif of the medal itself.

Naval Tropical Uniforms

The Pith Helmet

The naval pith helmet was identical to that for the Luftwaffe, being covered in tan cloth. The standard eagle and swastika shield badge was worn in gilt on black.

The Peaked Field Cap

A tropical peaked field cap was produced for the Navy which was identical in style to that of the Army, featuring a false flap. It was, however, made from tan cotton and had green cotton lining. The eagle and swastika insignia was in yellow-gold silk weave on a tan backing.

The Tropical Peaked Cap

Like the Luftwaffe, the Navy introduced a special tropical version of the Schirmmütze. In typical Navy style it featured a large peak and a leather chinstrap. It was made in tan-coloured cloth, including the stiffened peak, which lacked the gold embroidery which decorated that of the blue peaked cap. Insignia were of the standard naval style but in gold embroidery on tan rather than dark blue backing. Some officers and admirals wore chincords on this cap rather than the leather chinstrap.

The Tropical Field Blouse

The naval tropical field blouse was similar in style and cut to that of the Luftwaffe; but examples varied from a bright tan colour to a khaki brown. Pockets were in the Army style—pleated, with scalloped flaps, on early models and unpleated with straight flaps on later issues. The blouse could be buttoned up to the throat but was generally worn open. Buttons were a simplified version of the gilt anchor buttons worn on dark blue dress, having a fouled anchor in the centre, on a plain background, with a plain raised edge. These buttons were in olive- or tan-painted zinc. The cuffs differed from those on Luftwaffe and Army tropical field blouses in being non-adjustable.

The breast eagle was in golden yellow machine embroidery or machine woven silk on a tan background, though officers occasionally used the gilt metal pin-on breast eagle from the white naval summer tunic. Although most personnel seem to have worn the shoulder straps from their continental issue clothing on this field blouse, special tropical patterns were made. These were in tan coloured cloth and, for warrant officers, featured blue silk woven Tresse.

The Trousers
Extremely baggy tan tropical trousers in the Luftwaffe style were issued and worn with the tropical field blouse.

The Tropical Shirt
The naval tropical shirt was also in tan cotton, with two breast pockets, and was worn with a breast eagle and shoulder straps.

Personal Equipment Virtually the full range of equipment, i.e. belts, braces, some pouches, frogs, etc., was issued to troops bound for tropical service in a webbing rather than leather form, with metal equipment, such as gas mask containers, repainted in tan. Belt buckles were also issued painted in olive colour for tropical use. For details readers are directed to Osprey Men-at-Arms 234, *German Combat Equipments 1939–45*.

(NOTE. Steel helmets have not been described here as there was no special tropical version. Individual soldiers merely repainted the exterior of their helmets in tan coloured paint, often with sand mixed in to give a roughened effect and aid camouflage. The decal insignia were sometimes obscured, sometimes painted around.)

Other insignia
In general, trade badges, rank badges, etc., produced for the Afrikakorps were of identical design to their continental counterparts, but on an olive twill base rather than dark green or field grey wool; rank chevrons were copper-brown in place of silver-grey. Special insignia unique to the Afrikakorps were few and include the following;

Cuffbands
Prior to the introduction of the official formation cuffband for the Afrikakorps in July 1941, unofficial, privately made examples were already circulating. These were in black cloth with the legend 'Afrikakorps' machine embroidered in silver-grey thread block letters. This style can be encountered both with and without braid edging.

The official cufftitle was machine woven on a tan cloth band with a dark green central strip with aluminium weave bordering; the legend 'AFRIKAKORPS' in block letters was also executed in aluminium metallic weave. The band was 3.3 cm

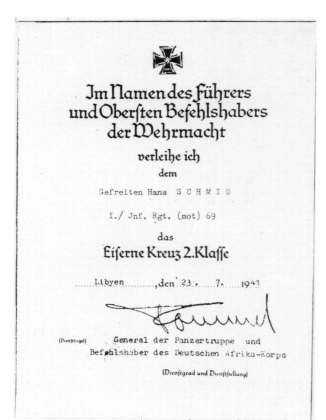

Award document for an Iron Cross 2nd Class, bearing Rommel's distinctive signature. He did not sign many such documents personally, a facsimile or rubber stamp version being used instead.

Officer's version of the Luftwaffe's 'Afrika' cuffband; the legend is hand-embroidered in aluminium thread on dark blue cloth. For other ranks the lettering would be in silver-grey cotton.

wide and was worn on the lower right sleeve. Although widely issued it was not always worn; it appears that many troops did not bother to attach it to their tunics. This cuffband could also be worn on the field grey continental uniform when home on leave.

The Luftwaffe also introduced its own African theatre cufftitle, to be worn by troops stationed in North Africa. This was in dark blue cloth, 3.3 cm wide, and bore the legend 'AFRIKA' in block letters, in silver-grey thread machine embroidery for other ranks and hand embroidered aluminium thread for officers. Before its introduction some Luftwaffe personnel wore, unofficially, the Army cuffband. In the Luftwaffe Museum in Uetersen there is displayed a variant of this cufftitle which is said to have belonged to the great Luftwaffe fighter ace Hans-Joachim Marseille. This piece has the legend in Gothic 'Frakturschrift', and the band is edged with black braid. Like its Army counterpart, the Luftwaffe cufftitle could be worn on the continental uniform when home on leave.

The Kriegsmarine is also known to have introduced an 'AFRIKA' cufftitle with the legend in yellow thread block letters (gold for officers), on a dark blue base. Photographic evidence exists to prove that this title was worn, but little is known about the regulations for issue, dimensions, materials, etc.

Campaign Decorations

In February 1943 Hitler ordered that the 'AFRIKA' cufftitles used by the Navy and Luftwaffe and the 'AFRIKAKORPS' title of the Army be replaced by a new title which would be accorded the status of a campaign decoration rather than a formation emblem.

This band was 3.3 cm wide and was in khaki brown camel hair material with the legend 'AFRIKA' in silver-grey letters, flanked by silver-grey stylised palm trees; the band was edged in silver-grey cotton braid. It was worn on the lower left sleeve.

To qualify for the cufftitle servicemen had to have served in North Africa for six months, or to have been wounded in action, or have contracted an illness in the theatre which required the recipient to be invalided home. All three requirements were waived if the recipient was killed in action, though in this case the next of kin received only the citation and not the actual cufftitle. Various amendments to the regulations were later made, such as the reduction of the qualifying period to four months for those who took part in the closing stages of the campaign.

Italo-German Campaign Medal

Introduced in early 1942, this decoration was actually an Italian award, yet only ever seems to have been awarded to German troops. It featured, on the obverse, two armoured knights, representing Germany and Italy, wrestling with the jaws of a crocodile, representing the British Empire. The reverse showed the Arco de Felini with a fasces to the left and a swastika to the right, all over the knot emblem of the House of Savoy. The legend 'Italo-German Campaign in Africa' in both languages was lettered

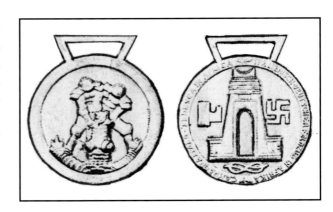

Obverse and reverse of the Italo-German medal for the African campaign, struck in bronze or bronzed zinc. Wear by German personnel was forbidden after the Italian Armistice of September 1943.

around the raised edge on the reverse. The ribbon was black/white/red/white/green, thus encompassing the national colours of both Italy and Germany. After 29 March 1944 an order was promulgated banning any further wear of Royal Italian military decorations.

THE PLATES

A: Uniform insignia

A1 The special tropical version of the Army collar patch was intended for wear by all ranks. It was woven in pale blue-grey artificial silk on a copper-brown backing, and lacked the Waffenfarbe stripe down the centre of each bar which was a feature of the Litzen on the field grey uniform at this period.

A2 The breast eagle pattern for the Army tropical tunic, woven in pale blue silk on an olive backing.

A3 The breast eagle pattern for the naval tropical tunic, machine woven in golden-yellow artificial silk on a tan backing.

A4 The Luftwaffe tropical breast eagle, machine embroidered in silver-grey cotton thread on a tan twill backing.

A5a The special arm badge for Sonderverband 288 in dark green silk weave with white and yellow details.

A5b The original silvered brass breast badge.

A6 The silk woven arm shield for members of the Deutsche-Arabische Lehr-Abteilung.

A7a The national colours shield, in metal alloy, common to the right side of the tropical helmet for all three armed services.

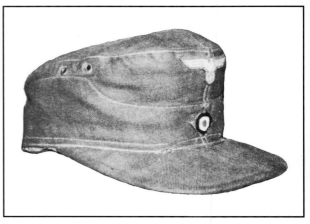

The best known item of tropical field dress: the Army other ranks' peaked field cap, made in dark olive material which could vary towards either brown or green with fading, and lined with bright red. Note the false flap; the two ventilation eyelets; the machine-woven eagle in pale blue-grey on tan, and the flat machine-woven national cockade on a diamond of tan backing. This late example lacks the Waffenfarbe soutache in an inverted V around the cockade.

A7b Left hand helmet shield for the Army, the details being in high relief.

A7c The left hand helmet shield for the Navy, details normally impressed.

A7d The left hand helmet badge for the Luftwaffe, the eagle flying towards the front of the helmet.

A8 The tropical version of the Mountain Troop arm badge, on a tan rather than the normal dark green backing.

A9 The tropical version of the SS cap insignia, in golden tan weave on a black backing.

B: Uniform insignia

B1 The first type (unofficial) 'Afrikakorps' cuffband, machine embroidered in silver-grey block letters on black cloth. These can be found both with and without silver-grey braid edging.

B2 The official 'Afrikakorps' formation cuffband, woven in aluminium thread on a dark green/tan background.

B3 The 'Afrika' campaign cufftitle, machine embroidered in silver-grey thread on a medium brown camel hair material. The braid edging is also silver grey.

The green-covered cork pith helmet, with brown leather strap and binding, and the right-hand white metal alloy badge painted with stripes of national colours.

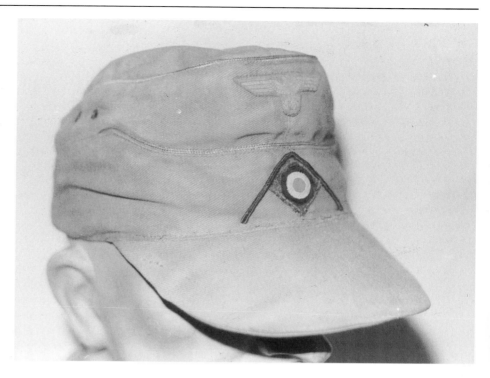

B4 The Luftwaffe's 'Afrika' cufftitle was machine embroidered in silver-grey thread for other ranks and hand embroidered in aluminium thread for officers, all on a blue backing.

B5 A known variant of the Luftwaffe 'Afrika' cufftitle has the legend in Gothic script and black braid edging.

B6 The Naval 'Afrika' cufftitle featured lettering embroidered in gold-coloured thread on a dark blue material.

B7 Other Ranks' and NCO's pattern tropical shoulder straps for the Army; the former bears Panzer pink Waffenfarbe, and the latter red Artillery Waffenfarbe. Note also the copper-brown NCO's Tresse.

B8 Other Ranks' and NCO's tropical shoulder straps for the Luftwaffe, similar to the Army's but in tan cloth. Yellow piping denotes flying personnel or paratroops, and red piping Flakartillerie.

B9 The rarely used Naval tropical shoulder straps were in tan cloth with blue Tresse for Warrant Officers. More usually, the straps from the dark blue or field grey naval uniforms were worn.

B10 Tropical SS shoulder straps, in black cloth but with copper-brown Tresse edging for NCOs. Shown here is the strap for an SS-Unterscharführer.

C: Vehicle insignia

Formation signs of the major units serving in North Africa. These were generally painted in white or yellow on the front glacis plate and rear hull of tanks, and on the front and rear fenders of soft skinned vehicles. Many vehicles arriving from Europe in the standard dark grey colour were suitably camouflaged or overpainted in sand colour, carefully avoiding the markings so that they still appeared on a dark grey background.

C1 Symbol in yellow carried on cadre vehicles from 3 Panzer Regiment absorbed in 5 leichte Division.

C2 Symbol carried by vehicles of 21 Panzer Division in white or yellow.

C3 Symbol carried by vehicles of 10 Panzer Division, in yellow.

C4 Symbol of 15 Panzer Division, usually in yellow or white when on grey background, and dark grey on sand yellow background.

C5 As well as the left hand symbol, in white, vehicles of 90 leichte Afrika Division also carried the DAK palm tree symbol over the individual vehicle's number.

C6 The emblem of 164 leichte Afrika Division, crossed swords over a map of Africa, in white.

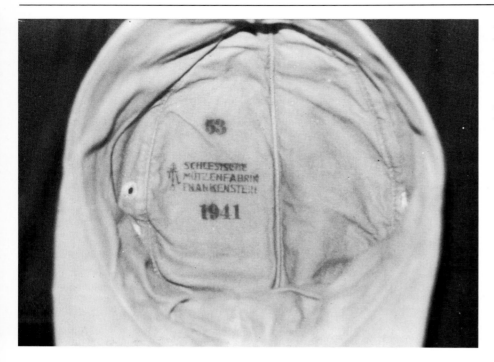

Interior of an other ranks' field cap, showing typical black-stamped markings on the scarlet cotton lining. Visible are the size '53', the manufacturer 'Schlesische Mützenfabrik' of Frankenstein, and the date '1941'. (E. L. Collection)

C7 The arrow emblem of 334 Infanterie Division, carried in white.

C8 The emblem of 999 leichte Division, usually carried in white.

C9 The emblem of the Ramcke Parachute Brigade, in black on white backing. The initial at bottom right is that of the individual battalion commander, in this case Kroh.

C10 The emblem of the Brandenburg unit in Africa, Abteilung von Koenen: a white pennant bearing black diamonds with white spots.

C11 The Hermann Göring Division used a 'clock' symbol to indicate the sub-unit. In the example given, a white disc bearing a red 'hand' in the 3 o'clock position indicates 3 Batterie, I/Flak Regiment 'HG'.

C12 The DAK symbol.

D1: Obergefreiter, Infantry

Newly arrived in North Africa, this junior NCO is wearing freshly issued tropical kit including the unpopular pith helmet, olive green tropical Feldbluse and breeches, and high leg lace-up boots. The waist-belt and bayonet frog are in webbing, though the ammunition pouches are the standard black leather pattern. The use of shirt and tie gives a formal appearance, in marked contrast to the typical desert veteran. Having seen service in earlier campaigns, the soldier wears the ribbon of the Iron Cross Second Class in his buttonhole, while on his left pocket are pinned the Infantry Assault Badge and black Wound Badge. His weapon is the standard Kar 98k carbine. On his left sleeve only is the double chevron of an Obergefreiter.

D2: Unteroffizier, Panzer troops

Divested of as much cumbersome clothing as possible, this Panzer crewman wears tropical shorts with high leg lace-up boots. In shirtsleeve order, the only insignia he shows are the shoulder straps showing his rank of Unteroffizier by the exact arrangement of the copper-coloured NCO Tresse, and his branch by the pink piping. In common with many of his comrades he has retained the M38 Feldmütze from his black Panzer service dress, bearing a pink Panzer Waffen-farbe soutache over the national cockade. Around his neck are worn one of the many variants of sun and sand goggles issued in North Africa.

D3: Feldwebel, Panzer troops

In contrast, this Feldwebel tank commander wears full tropical service dress. The Feldbluse has copper-brown NCO Tresse around the collar and the edge of the shoulder straps, which are also piped in pink and

A late-manufacture NCO's tropical field blouse; the unpleated pockets retain the scalloped flap, however. There is no Tresse round the collar, a not uncommon feature of late examples. (E. L. Collection)

carry a single aluminium rank pip. The aluminium skulls from the collar patches of the black Panzer jacket are worn on the lower lapels of the tropical Feldbluse. This NCO wears the ribbon of the Iron Cross Second Class in his buttonhole and the Panzer Battle Badge on his breast pocket. The waistbelt is the webbing type with olive painted buckle, from which is slung a Walther P38 pistol in a black leather holster. The tropical version of the M38 Feldmütze is worn, with its pink Waffenfarbe chevron. Long trousers and tropical ankle boots complete the uniform.

E1: Major, Aufklärungs-Abteilung 33

This major from an armoured recce unit of 15 Panzer Division wears the standard tropical Feldbluse to which have been added the hand embroidered collar patches from his field grey uniform; strips of golden yellow cavalry Waffenfarbe appear on the Litzen and the aluminium braid shoulder straps are sewn to a

golden yellow underlay. In this case, however, the standard all-ranks woven breast eagle has been retained. Tropical breeches are worn with high lace-up boots. A webbing belt is worn with the officer's pattern circular buckle; and note tropical issue shirt worn with a tie. The officer's version of the tropical M38 Feldmütze has a golden yellow cavalry soutache over the cockade; between the eagle and the cockade is pinned the gilt 'Schwedter Adler' dragoon tradition badge of Aufklärungs Abteilung 33, formed from Kavallerie Regiment 6. To his left breast pocket are pinned the Iron Cross First Class, and the Panzer Battle Badge in Bronze.

E2: Oberstleutnant, Infantry

Only occasionally seen worn with tropical dress was the standard peaked cap or Schirmmütze. This infantry officer wears his white-piped peaked cap, and has added the full set of continental insignia from his field grey dress to his tropical tunic. His rank of Oberstleutnant is indicated by a single gilt pip on the twisted matt grey braid shoulder strap. Normal continental issue black leather belt and holster are worn, as are black jackboots with the tropical breeches.

E3: Generalmajor

A general officer of the Afrikakorps resplendent in his

Late-model blouse of an Oberfeldwebel of Mountain Rifles, with the Gebirgsjäger right sleeve badge; note late-manufacture unpleated pockets with straight-cut flaps (E. L. Collection)

privately tailored version of the tropical Feldbluse. Of the same style as the standard pattern, it is cut in superior quality khaki brown woollen cloth and features turn-back cuffs. Full general's insignia from the field grey dress are displayed. His tropical Feldmütze has general's gilt piping and a gilt soutache over the cockade. Bright red general's Lampassen braid is sewn to the legs of the tropical breeches, and high lace-up boots are worn. This Generalmajor has been decorated with the 1939 Clasp to his 1914 Iron Cross First Class, and wears the Infantry Assault Badge; the German Cross in Gold is worn on the right breast pocket.

F1: Oberfeldwebel, Pioneers

An Oberfeldwebel of assault engineers fully equipped for battle. His M35 steel helmet has been overpainted in a tan colour mixed with sand to give it a rough finish. His Feldbluse collar bears NCO braid, and his shoulder straps are piped in the black Waffenfarbe of the Pioniere. As well as the webbing belt with olive-painted buckle the Oberfeldwebel wears webbing 'Y' straps and webbing ammunition pouches for his MP38/40 machine pistol. A hand grenade is tucked into his waistbelt ready for instant use. His decorations include the Iron Cross Second and First Class, the silver Wound Badge and the

General Assault Badge. Long trousers and ankle boots are worn.

F2: Unteroffizier, Pioneers

The Oberfeldwebel's comrade, an Unteroffizier, wears a similar uniform, but is armed with a Kar 98k carbine. This rear view clearly shows the various items of kit which make up the soldier's basic combat load.

F3: Obergefreiter, Artillery

This soldier is dressed for night guard duty in the tropical greatcoat of heavy brown wool, to protect him from the cold of the desert night; similar to its field grey counterpart, it lacks the contrasting collar. This Obergefreiter from an Artillery unit wears long trousers tucked into ankle boots. Armed with a Kar 98k, he wears the webbing belt but with black leather ammunition pouches. His steel helmet has been carefully repainted in sand paint, avoiding the original helmet decals; few soldiers bothered to be so careful.

G1: Leutnant, Luftwaffe Flakartillerie

A Luftwaffe Flak officer wearing the Army pattern tropical Feldbluse as was often the case before Luftwaffe tropical kit became generally available. The tunic retains its original Army breast eagle but has the correct Luftwaffe shoulder straps for this rank and branch in bright silver braid on a red base. The collar patches from continental blue-grey service uniform, in silver embroidery on red, have also been added. The officer also wears Army issue tropical breeches and high laced boots. The tunic pocket bears the Luftwaffe Flak War Badge, and the ribbon of the Iron Cross Second Class is worn in the buttonhole. The standard Luftwaffe M35 blue-grey steel helmet, overpainted sand colour, still shows its Luftwaffe insignia.

G2: Hauptmann fighter pilot, Luftwaffe Fliegertruppe

This casually dressed Luftwaffe fighter pilot wears a short-sleeved shirt in Luftwaffe tan bearing the shoulder straps for a Hauptmann of Fliegertruppe— silver braid with two gilt pips on a golden yellow base. The Luftwaffe breast eagle, in silver-grey on a tan triangular base, is the type common to all ranks. On the shirt pocket is pinned his Iron Cross First Class and Pilot/Observer's Badge. Tropical shorts are worn

Detail of NCO collar Tresse, in a warm, golden copper-brown; 'all ranks' collar Litzen, in blue-grey artificial silk weave with reddish-tan central void and 'lights' down the bars; olive shoulder strap with Tresse all round edge, two silver-grey metal pips, and outer piping in the light green of the Gebirgsjäger. (E. L. Collection)

Details of the regulation issue olive tropical breeches, worn by all ranks with the high-leg laced tropical boots. Note lacing at the lower leg, zinc fly buttons, and white canvas reinforcement inside the waistband; the fob pocket is just visible left of the second button. (E. L. Collection)

with ankle boots over which his socks are rolled. Use in Africa of the blue-grey Schirmmütze was quite common.

G3: Oberstleutnant, Luftwaffe Fliegertruppe

This Oberstleutnant and Geschwader-Kommodore wears the Luftwaffe tropical Feldbluse. His rank is shown only by shoulder straps in bright silver twisted braid, with single gilt pip, on a golden yellow underlay. No collar patches are worn; and the breast eagle in this case is the aluminium pin-back type. On his right cuff is the Luftwaffe 'Afrika' cuffband in aluminium thread hand embroidery for officers. Loose trousers are worn with ankle boots. This officer has elected to wear the white-topped summer pattern of the peaked service cap in place of the blue-grey continental pattern.

H1: Jäger, Fallschirmjäger-Brigade Ramcke, 1942

A Luftwaffe paratrooper from the Ramcke Brigade wearing the jump-smock in 'splinter' pattern camouflage material, over the standard Luftwaffe tropical trousers, and front-lacing jump-boots. The waistbelt is in webbing material with an olive-painted Luftwaffe buckle. Around the neck is worn a tan cloth rifle ammunition bandolier. In the desert heat the smock is worn with the neck open and the sleeves rolled. The paratroop issue steel helmet is over-painted in a tan colour. The weapon is the standard Kar 98k carbine.

H2: Oberfeldwebel, Panzer-Regiment 'Hermann Göring', 1943

A senior NCO from the 'Hermann Göring' Division shows an interesting combination of clothing and insignia. He wears the Luftwaffe tropical Feldbluse without collar patches, his rank Oberfeldwebel being shown by the tan shoulder straps with copper-brown braid edging and a single pip; the pink piping indicates that he is from an armoured unit of the Division. On the lower right cuff is the NCO's pattern of the pre-1942 'General Göring' cufftitle, widely retained after the introduction of later patterns. Luftwaffe trousers are worn tucked into ankle boots. The cap is an exact copy of the Army pattern but in tan rather than olive cloth and with Luftwaffe insignia. On the left side of this particular cap is worn an alloy SS pattern cap deathshead badge, a fashion known within the division's Panzer-Regiment.

H3: Leutnant, Jäger-Regiment 'Hermann Göring', 1943

Conversing with the Oberfeldwebel is a young officer

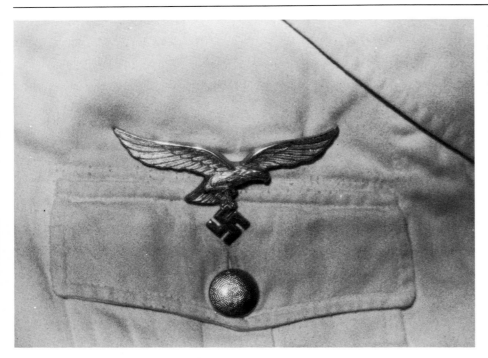

Luftwaffe officer's pin-back aluminium breast eagle, worn in Europe on the white summer tunic, here applied to the tropical field blouse. (E. L. Collection)

from the Jäger Regiment. The combination of clothing shown seems unusual but is known from photographic evidence. The cap worn is the unique Luftwaffe 'Hermann Meyer' with buttoned neck flap. Over the standard tropical shirt is worn a Waffen-SS camouflage smock of first pattern 'plane tree' type, commonly used by the division. The usual baggy trousers and ankle boots are worn. A leather belt with double-claw buckle supports a Walther P38 pistol in a leather holster.

I1: Bootsman, Kriegsmarine, shore duty

A Navy seaman guarding one of Rommel's supply ports. He wears a combination of field grey and tan tropical clothing. Naval issue tropical trousers were of almost identical appearance to those of the Luftwaffe, being cut very loose, but lacked the thigh pocket. Black leather marching boots are worn. The tunic is from the field grey uniform and is similar to that of the Army, differing mainly in having slash rather than patch lower pockets. The collar has been pressed open. Shoulder straps cut in field grey cloth are wide and with pointed ends; they bear the emblem of the sailor's trade—crossed anchors—in yellow cotton embroidery. The breast eagle is in woven yellow silk on a green backing, and the field grey buttons bear the traditional anchor motif. Black

leather ammunition pouches for the sailor's Kar 98k are worn on a black leather waistbelt with gilt buckle. The tropical field cap is identical in appearance to that of the Army but in tan cloth with the national emblem in a yellow silk on tan base.

I2: Kapitänleutnant, Kriegsmarine

A naval officer in full tropical dress. He wears the standard naval tropical Feldbluse, a four-pocket open-neck tunic very similar to that of the Luftwaffe; colours varied from golden tan to a medium brown. Shoulder straps, in silver braid with two gilt pips on a dark blue underlay, indicate the rank. He has attached a gilt metal pin-on breast eagle to his tunic in place of the standard woven pattern. Tan breeches are worn with black leather jackboots.

The naval tropical peaked cap was rarely encountered. It closely followed the design of the dark blue Schirmmütze but was cut entirely in a tan twill material, with a brown leather chinstrap and golden-yellow-on-tan insignia. The belt is brown leather with a gilt double-claw buckle.

I3: Stabsteuermann, Kriegsmarine

A warrant officer serving on a patrol vessel operating from a North African port. He wears the tan naval issue tropical shirt, with shoulder straps and all-ranks reast eagle; typically, the rank shoulder straps from he navy blue uniform have been applied. The breast agle is in yellow thread on a tan backing. On the reast pocket are pinned the Iron Cross First Class nd the Minesweeper's War Badge. Tropical issue horts are worn with the standard black leather waist-elt with gilt buckle. In this example the white ummer issue sidecap is worn, bearing its blue-on-hite insignia.

1: Oberfeldwebel, Sonderverband 288

He wears full Army tropical issue dress including a te pattern peaked field cap without Waffenfarbe outache. His tunic also lacks the usual NCO collar 'resse, common in later stages of the campaign when upplies were erratic. The tunic had been simplified y the removal of the pocket pleats and the scallop to ne flaps. His shoulder straps retain the NCO braid, nd bear the single rank pip of his rank; green outer iping indicates the grenadier branch. On the upper ght sleeve is the silk woven emblem of Sonderver-and 288. The waistbelt is in olive webbing with an live-painted buckle. Olive breeches are worn with igh lace-up boots.

2: Stabsfeldwebel, Feldgendarmerie

smart warrant-officer of the Feldgendarmerie in nirtsleeve order and shorts. The shirt has been eatly pressed and has the sleeves rolled. His shoul-er straps in olive cloth with copper-brown Tresse ature orange-red branch piping and the three pips f his rank. Shorts are worn with a webbing waistbelt earing an olive-painted buckle. Ankle boots are orn with the socks neatly rolled over the top. The tabsfeldwebel wears the early pattern Army pith elmet in cork covered with olive canvas. Around the ck is worn the Feldgendarmerie duty gorget.

3: Sonderführer

erhaps anticipating language problems, the Feld-endarmerie warrant-officer is accompanied by a onderführer interpreter. Of officer status, he wears e aluminium-piped version of the peaked field cap ith a soutache in the grey-blue Waffenfarbe of the onderführer officials. In place of the normal tropical ollar tabs he wears the special patches of this officer's anch of service; these have a blue-grey base with a lver braid bar, with one end cut straight and the

Hauptmann Sandrock of the 'Hermann Göring' Division wearing Luftwaffe tropical uniform; note divisional cufftitle on his right sleeve, and 'Afrika' campaign cufftitle on his left sleeve. (Sandrock)

other pointed. The shoulder straps have blue-grey underlay with silver braid incorporating a red/black fleck. On the lower left sleeve is the 'Afrikakorps' formation cufftitle. A tropical webbing belt is worn with the circular officer's buckle in olive painted zinc or aluminium. Breeches and long lace-up boots are worn. On the right breast pocket is worn the War Merit Cross First Class.

K1: Freiwilliger, Deutsche-Arabische Lehr-Abteilung

A volunteer from the 'Free Arabian Corps', this soldier wears the turban with his tropical Feldbluse. On the upper right sleeve is sewn the 'Freies Arabien' shield. Tropical breeches are worn but with puttees and ankle boots. Initially, before the issue of German tropical dress, French uniforms were worn together with a white armband bearing the legend 'Im Dienst der deutschen Wehrmacht' in black lettering.

K2: Army Protestant chaplain

A military chaplain in formal tropical dress as for burial services, etc. The officer's version of the peaked field cap bears a Waffenfarbe soutache in the violet colour of the Army chaplaincy. Officer's collar tabs from the field grey dress are worn, in aluminium hand embroidery with violet Waffenfarbe. No shoulder straps are worn on the chaplain's uniform. The breast eagle, also from the field grey uniform, is in aluminium hand embroidery on a dark green backing. On a long chain around the neck is worn a plain cross indicating a Protestant chaplain; a Catholic priest would have used a crucifix bearing the figure of Christ. On the left sleeve is worn a chaplain's white armband bearing a violet stripe and a red cross.

K3: SS-Untersturmführer, Einsatzkommando Tunis

This, admittedly speculative, illustration shows how the staff of SS/SD Einsatzkommando Tunis would presumably have appeared in tropical SS service dress. The tropical peaked cap is very plain with no false flaps, and bears the individual SS eagle and skull

Kriegsmarine tropical tunic, in tan cotton with partial white cotton lining. The warrant officer's shoulder straps are the blue and gold pattern from the continental uniform; use of actual tropical shoulder straps, in tan with blue Tresse, was not common. (E. L. Collection,

adges in tan silk weave on black. The tunic is the talian 'Sahariana' style, favoured by some German fficers. The sleeve eagle is also woven in tan on black nd on the lower left sleeve is the diamond-shaped rm patch bearing the silver letters SD. No collar atches are worn. The waistbelt is the standard black ather pattern with SS issue buckle. Long tan ousers are worn tucked into short ankle boots.

1: Nurse, German Red Cross

Jurses of the German Red Cross served with allantry and distinction on many fronts and North frica was no exception. This nurse wears full opical kit. On the front of a puggaree added to the n coloured sun helmet has been pinned the enamel- d Red Cross brooch normally worn at the throat. he tan cotton tunic existed in both long and short- eeved versions. Note the top pocket flaps are stened by one button whereas the lower have two. A n cloth belt is worn; and the right sleeve features the hite-on-grey silk woven DRK emblem with 'Berlin

Detail of the Kriegsmarine warrant officer's tropical tunic, showing golden yellow machine-woven silk breast eagle on triangular tan backing. The brown-painted zinc buttons have plain raised borders rather than the roped borders of the gilt buttons used on continental uniform. Note armpit ventilation holes. (E. L. Collection)

1' area identification. A pleated tan skirt is worn with black stockings and shoes. The ribbon of the Iron Cross in the second buttonhole of the tunic shows that she has been decorated for bravery in tending wounded soldiers under fire.

L2: Driver, 4th Motor Transport Regiment, NSKK

One of the smaller units to serve in North Africa was the 4th Motor Transport Regiment of the NSKK or National Socialist Motor Transport Corps, a branch of the Nazi Party. Engaged in auxiliary transport duties, they wore Luftwaffe tropical clothing. The driver shown here wears the Luftwaffe sun helmet but with a silver-on-black woven NSKK eagle on the

Rommel with German and Italian officers; behind him stands Oberst Diesener, at extreme right Gen. Gause, and at left sits Gen. Navarini. Behind the Italian general stands a Sonderführer interpreter: note collar patches. (Josef Charita)

Although the ubiquitous 'jerrycan' was used for carrying water as well as petrol, marked with a bold white-painted cross, drinking water containers were also supplied to the DAK. This 10 litre example is of sand-painted aluminium, with the legend 'Trinkwasser 10 1' stencilled in white. (E. L. Collection)

left side. In shirtsleeve order, he wears the single right hand shoulder strap of an NSKK private, in silver and black twist cord on a black base. On the left sleeve is the NSKK sleeve eagle, identical to that worn on the sun helmet. A brown leather belt with double-claw buckle is worn with the tropical shorts and ankle boots.

L3: TN-Vormann, Technisches Nothilfe
A number of personnel from the Technical Emergency Service or TeNo served in North Africa alongside the Luftwaffe on airfield construction and

repair; Luftwaffe tropical clothing was worn. This junior NCO wears the sidecap with Luftwaffe insignia, and the Luftwaffe field blouse with added TeNo shoulder straps, collar patches and sleeve eagle; the machine woven grey-on-black 'Technisches Nothilfe' cuffband is worn on the lower left sleeve. A Luftwaffe belt supports a holstered Walther P38. Long trousers are worn tucked into ankle boots.

Notes sur les planches en couleur

A Insigne d'uniforme.
A1 Insigne de col sur la tunique tropicale, tous les grades, toutes les branches. **A2** Insigne de poitrine porté du côté droit sur la tunique tropicale de l'armée terrestre, tous les grades, toutes les branches. **A3** Insigne de la Marine sur la tunique tropicale. **A4** Insigne de l'Armée de l'Air sur la tunique tropicale. **A5a** Insigne de manche, SVb 288. **A5b** L'une des premières versions en métal. **A6** Insigne de manche, bataillon allemand-arabe. **A7a** Insigne de casque, côté droit. **A7b** Insigne de casque de l'armée terrestre, côté gauche. **A7c** Insigne de casque de la Marine, côté gauche. **A7d** Insigne de casque de l'Armée de l'Air, côté guache. **A8** Insigne de manche, troupes alpines, version tropicale. **A9** Insigne de coiffure SS, version tropicale.

B Insigne d'uniforme.
B1 L'une des premières bandes de tissu non officielles sur le revers de la manche indiquant l'Afrikakorps. **B2** Bande de tissu officielle sur le revers de la manche. **B3** Bande de tissu sur le revers de la manche de la campagne d'Afrique. **B4** Bande de tissu de l'Armée de l'Air sur le revers de la manche. **B5** Variante non officielle. **B6** Bande de tissu de campagne de la Marine sur le revers de la manche. **B7** Pattes d'épaule caractéristiques, tunique tropicale, de l'Armée; simple soldat, troupes blindées, et sous-officiers, artillerie. **B8** Equivalences de l'Armée de l'Air, de la branche d'aviation et de l'artillerie anti-aérienne. **B9** Pattes d'épaule tropicales de la Marine rarement utilisées avec tresse bleue pour les adjudants. **B10** Patte d'épaule tropicale, SS, avec Tresse brun cuivré pour les sous-officiers.

C Insigne de véhicule.
C1 Div. 3. Pz. (5 leichte Div.). **C2** Div. 21. Pz. **C3** Div. 10. Pz. **C4** Div. 15. Pz. **C5** Afrika-Div. 90 le. **C6** Af. Div. 164 le. **C7** Div. Inf. 334. **C8** Div. le. 999. **C9** Brigade de Parachutiste Ramcke. **C10** Abt. von Koenen, Brandenburg. **C11** Style d'insigne de la Div. 'Hermann Göring' ici Groupe d'artillerie 3 Regt I/artillerie anti-aérienne. 'HG'. **C12** Afrikakorps.

D1 Uniforme tropical réglementaire d'officier subalterne, porté par un nouvel arrivé en Afrique. **D2** L'ensemble comprenant une chemise (avec insigne seulement sur les pattes d'épaule de la tunique), des shorts, les premières bottes tropicales lacées, et son calot noir de l'uniforme européen était plus courant pour les équipages de char, 1941. **D3** Un ensemble plus élégant avec tunique tropicale, pantalons longs et bottillons, pour Feldwebel. La tresse de grade des sous-officiers, de couleur marron, se portait sur haut du col et sur les pattes d'épaule; les Waffenfarbe roses sur les pattes d'épaule et la coiffure identifient la branche; notez les cranes de métal des insignes de col des uniformes européens épinglés en bas du col.

E1 Feldmütze tropical d'officier avec un liseré – notez l'insigne traditionnel de cette unité, l'aigle du dragon' du Kavallerie-Regt 6. Les Waffenfarbe jaunes de la cavalerie apparaissent également sur les pattes d'épaule et les insignes de col de l'uniforme européen, les officiers portaient souvent ces derniers sur les tuniques tropicales et toujours les premiers. Notez la boucle du ceinturon de cet officier. **E2** Le Schirmmütze gris des troupes allemandes ne se portait parfois, mais pas fréquemment avec la tenue tropicale en Afrique – il en est de même pour les bottes à genouillères noires. **E3** Version confectionnée dans le privé d'un uniforme tropical en laine marron, avec insigne de général de l'uniforme européen.

F1 Equipement complet de combat en toile et casque d'acier peint couleur de sable, ils sont portés par un sous-officier du génie d'assaut – notez les Waffenfarbe noires. **F2** Vue de dos de l'équipement, il est porté ici par un officier subalterne armé d'un fusil. **F3** Manteau tropical en laine marron. Il était fréquent de rencontrer une alliance de l'équipement en toile et des cartouchières en cuir distribuées en Europe.

G1 Officier de l'artillerie anti-aérienne de l'Armée de l'Air portant une tunique de l'Armée terrestre avant que soit distribuée une tunique équivalente pour l'Armée de l'Air; notez qu'on a conservé l'insigne de poitrine de l'Armée terrestre auquel ont été ajoutés les insignes d'épaule et de col de l'uniforme européen de l'Armée de l'Air. **G2** Aigle pour tous les grades sur la poitrine de la chemise à manche courte avec insignes de l'uniforme européen de grade et de branche ajoutés sur les pattes d'épaule, ainsi que décorations; le calot bleu européen était souvent utilisé en Afrique. **G3** La tunique tropicale réglementaire de l'Armée de l'Air n'avait pas d'insignes de col; les officiers portaient souvent un aigle en métal fixé par une épingle sur la poitrine. Notez la bande de tissu 'Afrika' de style officier sur le revers de la manche et la Schirmmütze d'été dont le haut est blanc.

H1 Combinaison de camouflage dont le motif représente des 'éclats d'obus' avec pantalons réglementaires tropicaux de l'Armée de l'Air; notez la coupe ample et la poche sur la cuisse gauche; ceinturon et bandoulière à cartouches tropicaux; et casque en acier peint couleur sable des parachutistes. **H2** Les 'modes' régimentaires comprenaient l'addition d'un insigne SS portant un crane sur le côté de la casquette, ici une version de l'Armée de l'Air couleur kaki pâle de la casquette de toile à visière couleur olive de l'Armée terrestre. Tunique tropicale de l'Armée de l'Air, avec seulement des pattes d'épaule comme identification de grade et de branche; et bande de tissu 'Général Göring' sur le revers de la manche, modèle pré-1942 pour sous-officier souvent conservé en 1943–44. **H3** Un uniforme très mélangé confirmé par

Farbtafeln

A Uniformabzeichen
A1 Tropenblusen-Abzeichen – alle Ränge, alle Waffengattungen. **A2** Tropen-bluse, Abzeichen rechte Brustseite, alle Ränge & Gattungen. **A3** Marinetropen-bluse, Abzeichen. **A4** Luftwaffen-Tropenbluse, Abzeichen. **A5a** Armabzeichen, SVb 288. **A5b** Ursprüngliche Metallversion. **A6** Armabzeichen, Deutsch-ara-bische Abteilung. **A7a** Helmabzeichen, rechts. **A7b** Infanteriehelm-Abzeichen, links. **A7c** Marinehelm-Abzeichen, links. **A7d** Luftwaffenhelm-Abzeichen, links. **A8** Armabzeichen, Gebirgsjäger, Tropenversion. **A9** SS-Kappenabzeichen, Tropenversion.

B Uniformabzeichen
B1 Frühes inoffizielles Manschettenband des Afrikakorps. **B2** Offizielles Manschettenband. **B3** Afrikakampagne-Manschettenband. **B4** Luftwaffen-Manschettenband. **B5** Inoffizielle Version. **B6** Marinekampagne-Manschettenband. **B7** Typische Schulterstücke, Armee-Tropenbluse; Soldat, Panzerkorps; Unteroffizier, Artillerie. **B8** Luftwaffen-Äquivalente, Fallschirmjäger und Flakartillerie. **B9** Selten verwendete, tropische Marine-Schulteraufschläge mit blauer Borte für Deckoffiziere. **B10** Tropen-Schulterstücke, SS, mit kupferbrauner Tresse für Unteroffiziere.

C Fahrzeugabzeichen
C1 3. Panzerdivision (5 leichte Divisionen). **C2** 21. Panzerdivision. **C3** 10. Panzerdivision. **C4** 15. Panzerdivision. **C5** 90 leichte Afrika-Division. **C6** 164 leichte Afrika-Division. **C7** 334 Infanterie-Division. **C8** 999 leichte Division. **C9** Ramcke-Fallschirmjägerbrigade. **C10** Abteilung von Koenen, Brandenburg. **C11** Abzeichen der Hermann Göring-Division, hier 3. Batterie, I/Flak-Regiment 'HG'. **C12** Afrikakorps.

D1 Dienstuniform eines Obergefreiten, neu in Afrika eingetroffen. **D2** Üblicher für Panzerbesatzungen, 1941, war diese Kombination von Feldbluse (Schulterstücke als einziges Abzeichen), Shorts, die frühen hohen Schnürstiefel und schwarze Feldkappe von der europäischen Uniformversion. **D3** Elegantere Kombination von Tropen-Feldbluse, langer Hose und kurzen Tropenstiefeln und Tropen-Feldmütze. Braune Tresse als Rangabzeichen für Feldwebel, getragen nm Kragenrand Schulter-stücken; rosa Waffenfarbe an Schulterstücken und Mütze identifiziert die Waffengattung; sie metallner Totenkopf vom europäischen Uniformkragen jetzt am unteren Kragenrand.

E1 Tropen-Feldmütze eines Majors – sie traditionelles Abzeichen dieser Einheit, den 'Schwedter Adler' der Dragoner des 6. Kavallerieregiments. Die gelbe Waffenfarbe scheint auch auf den Schulterstücken und Kragenabzeichen auf, stammend von der europäischen Uniformversion; die Kragenabzeichen wurde oft von Offizieren an den Tropen-Feldblusen angebracht, die Schulterstücke immer. Man beachte die Gürtelschnalle. **E2** Die feldgraue Schirmmütze wurde manchmal, aber nicht oft mit der Tropenuniform in Afrika getragen, dasselbe trifft auf die schwarzen Stiefel zu. **E3** Privat geschneiderte Version der Tropenuniform in braunem Wollstoff mit Rangabzeichen eines generals von der europäischen Uniform.

F1 Komplette Kampfausrüstung mit Segeltuchgurten und sandfarbenem Stahlhelm, getragen von einem Oberfeldwebel der Pioniere – siehe schwarze Waffenfarbe. **F2** Rückenansicht der Ausrüstung, hier getragen von einem gewehrtragenden Unteroffizier. **F3** Langer Tropenmantel aus braunem Wollstoff. Kombination von Gurten und europäischen Taschen usw. war nicht unüblich.

G1 Ein Luftwaffenleutnant der Flakartillerie mit Armee-feldbluse, bevor noch die entsprechende Luftwaffen-feldbluse ausgegeben wurde; Armeeabzeichen an der Brust beibehalten, zusätzlich aber Abzeichen der Luftwaffe an Kragen und Schulterstücken, wie bei europäischer Uniform. **G2** Allen Rängen gemeinsamer Luftwaffenadler an der Brust des kurzärmeligen Hemdes, mit Schulterstücken für Rang- und Waffengattungsabzeichen; süzätliche Auszeichnungen; die blaue europäische Kappe wurde oft in Afrika getragen. **G3** Die tropische Standard-Feldbluse der Luftwaffe hatte keine Kragenabzeichen; die Offiziere trugen oft einen ansteckbaren Metalladler an der Brust. Siehe 'Afrika'-Manschettenband für Offiziere sowie Sommer-Schirmmütze mit weißem Kopf.

H1 Tarnjacke mit 'Splitter'-Muster und Luftwaffen-Tropenhose, bauschig geschnitten, mit Tasch am linken Schenkel; Tropengürtel und Bandolier, sandfarbiger Stahlhelm. **H2** Zur Regimentsmode gehörte ein zusätzlicher SS-Totenkopf an der Seite der Mütze, hier ein hell-khakifarbene Luftwaffenversion der oliv-farbenen Armeemütze. Luftwaffen-Tropenfeldbluse, auf der nur Schulterstücke Rang und Waffengattung anzeigen; das 'General Göring'-Manschettenband für Unteroffiziere stammt aus der Zeit vor 1942, wurde jedoch zwischen 1943–44 oft beibehalten. **H3** Stark gemischte Uniform, durch Fotos bestätigt; die Tarnjacke der Waffen-SS war in der 'HG'-Division weit verbreitet; die Schirmkappe wurde 'hermann Meyer' genannt und war mit ihrem anknöpfbaren Nackenschutz nur bei der Luftwaffe zu finden.

I1 Kombination von feldgrauen und tropischen Uniformstücken der Marine;

des photographies: la combinaison de camouflage des Waffen-SS était très répandue dans la Div. 'HG'; la casquette de toile à visière est le modèle 'Hermann Meyer', unique à l'Armée de l'Air, avec rabat sur le cou qui se boutonnait.

I1 Combinaison de pièces en gris particulier aux troupes allemandes et de pièces tropicals distribuées dans la Marine; pantalon tropical de la Marine auxquel manquait la poche sur la cuisse du pantalon de l'Armée de l'Air; les casquettes tropicales en toile et à visière de la Marine étaient la version kaki pâle de l'Armée terrestre. **I2** L'uniforme tropical de grande tenue rarement porté mais réglementaire pour officier de la Marine à terre; notez en particulier la Schirmmütze kaki, unique à la Marine. **I3** Chemise tropicale de la Marine avec pattes d'épaule bleues de grade et de branche de l'uniforme européen, et 'casquette d'abordage' (Bordmütze) blanche pour l'été.

J1 Uniforme de grande tenue tropical de l'armée terrestre, un modèle plus tardif au style simplifié sans les plis sur les poches ou la Tresse de col, et sans les chevrons Waffenfarbe sur la casquette. Notez l'insigne de l'unité sur la manche droite. **J2** Un uniforme élégant avec shorts et chemise à manche courte, casque en sola et hausse-col de la police militaire, ce dernier indiquant qu'il est en service. **J3** Peut-être un interprète; son statut de fonctionnaire de l'armée est indiqué par les Waffenfarbe bleues-grises, le liseré d'argent sur la casquette, et les insignes spéciaux de col et sur les pattes d'épaule.

K1 A l'origine un ancien uniforme français avait été distribué; par la suite tenue tropicale des troupes allemandes avec bandes molletières. Les turbans furent remplacés par des casquettes de toile pour une partie du personnel. Notez l'insigne sur la manche de cette organisation. **K2** Uniforme tropical de cérémonie, avec Waffenfarbe violettes d'aumôniers, pas de pattes d'épaule, brassard d'aumônier, et croix protestante sur une chaîne. **K3** Une reconstitution fondée sur des hypothèses de tenue du menu personnel SS/SD, elle repose sur des photographes prises en Corse. Notez le style saharienne pour la tunique de type italien.

L1 Uniforme tropical réglementaire; des versions à manche courte et manche longue existaient. L'insigne de manche DRK indiquait la région d'origine. Notez le ruban avec la croix de fer – les infirmières DRK recevaient une décoration pour soigner les blessés sous le feu. **L2** Fondamentalement un uniforme tropical de l'armée de l'air avec insigne portant l'aigle des NSKK sur le casque et la manche, et une seule patte d'épaule de grade NSKK. **L3** Le personnel militaire qui assurait l'entretien sur le champ d'aviation portait l'uniforme de l'armée de l'air; notez les pattes d'épaule ajoutées TeNo, les insignes de col, l'aigle sur la manche et la bande de tissu sur le revers de la manche.

Marine-Tropenhose, ohne Schenkeltasche der Luftwaffe; tropische Marine-Schirm-kappe, Hell-khaki-Version der Armeekappe. **I2** Selten gesehen, aber vorschriftsmäßige Galauniform für Marineoffiziere an Land; siehe besonder die khaki Schirmmütze, nur für die Marine. **I3** Marine-Tropenhemß mit blauen Schulteraufschlägen für Rang un Waffengattung von der europäischen Uniform, mit weißer Sommer-Bordmütze.

J1 Volle Armee-Tropenuniform in späterem, vereinfachten Stil, ohne Taschenfalten oder Kragentresse, auch ohne Waffenfarben-Winkel auf der Mütze. Siehe Abzeichen der Einheit am rechten Ärmel. **J2** Säuberliche Uniform mit kurzen Ärmeln und Shorts, Korkhelm und Schild der Militärpolizei, was zeigt, daß er sich im Dienst befindet. **J3** Vielleicht ein Dolmetscher; sein Status als Armeefunktionär wird durch die blaugraue Waffenfarbe, Mützenpaspel in Silber und spezielle Kragenabzeichen und Schulterstücke angezeigt.

K1 Ursprünglich wurden alte französische Uniformen ausgegeben, später dann deutsche Tropenuniformen mit Wickelgamaschen. Siehe Ärmelabzeichen dieser Einheit. **K2** Formelle Tropenuniform eines Feldkaplans, Waffenfarbe Violett, ohne Schulterstücke, Feldkaplan-Schild und umgehängtes Kreuz ohne Christus-figur (protestantisch). **K3** Spekulative Rekonstruktion der Uniform einer kleinen SS/SD-Einheit in Tunis, beruhend auf Fotos von Personal in Korsika. Siehe 'Shahariana'-Feldbluse nach italienischer Art.

L1 Vorschriftsmäßige Tropenuniform; es gab versionen mit kurzen und mit langen Ärmeln. Das DRK-Ärmelabzeichen gibt Herkunftsland an. Siehe Ordens-band für Eisernes Kreuz – DRK-Schwestern wurden oft dafür ausgezeichnet, Verwundete unter Beschuß versorgt zu haben. **L2** Grundlegende Luftwaffen-Tropenuniform mit NSKK-Adlerabzeichen an Helm und Ärmel und einem Schulter-stück für NSKK-Rang. **L3** Dieses Bodenpersonal für Flugplatzwartung trug Luftwaffenuniform; siehe zusätzliche Schulterstücke mit TeNo-Aufschrift, Kragenabzeichen, Adlerabzeichen und Manschettenband am Ärmel.